# POWERFUL WOMEN

# POWERFUL WOMEN

## *Dancing on the Glass Ceiling*

### SAM PARKHOUSE

JOHN WILEY & SONS, LTD

Chichester · New York · Weinheim · Brisbane · Singapore · Toronto

*Other Wiley Editorial Offices*

John Wiley & Sons, Inc., 605 Third Avenue,
New York, NY 10158-0012, USA

WILEY-VCH Verlag GmbH, Pappelallee 3,
D-69469 Weinheim, Germany

John Wiley & Sons Australia Ltd, 33 Park Road, Milton,
Queensland 4064, Australia

John Wiley & Sons (Asia) Pte Ltd, 2 Clementi Loop #02-01,
Jin Xing Distripark, Singapore 129809

John Wiley & Sons (Canada) Ltd, 22 Worcester Road,
Rexdale, Ontario M9W 1L1, Canada

***British Library Cataloguing in Publication Data***
A catalogue record for this book is available from the British Library

ISBN 0–471–49905–6

Typeset in Garamond ITC from the author's disks
by Florence Production Ltd, Stoodleigh, Devon

Printed and bound in Great Britain by Biddles Ltd, Guildford and
King's Lynn

This book is printed on acid-free paper responsibly manufactured from
sustainable forestry, in which at least two trees are planted for each one
used for paper production.

# Contents

# Key Players

Kate Bleasdale (Match Group; Medicentres)
Barbara Cassani (Chief Executive of Go Airlines)
Janie Dear (Soup Opera)
Belinda Earl (Debenhams)
Clara Freeman (Marks & Spencer; Opportunity Now)
Jan Hall (Institute of Directors; Spencer Stuart)
Rachael Heyhoe Flint (MCC; Wolverhampton Wanders FC)
Beverley Hodson (WHSmith)
Nicola Horlick (Société Générale)
Lady Elspeth Howe (Equal Opportunities; Broadcasting
    Standards)
Ann Iverson (ex head of Laura Ashley)
Baroness Margaret Jay (Minister for Women)
Karen Jones (Café Rouge; Punch Taverns)
Denise Kingsmill (Competition Commission)
Martha Lane Fox (lastminute.com)
Lesley MacDonagh (Lovells)
Dame Barbara Mills QC (former Director of Public
    Prosecutions; head of Forum UK)
Sally O'Sullivan (ex IPC; Cabal Communications)
Fiona Price (Fiona Price & Partners)
Gail Rebuck (Random House)
Anita Roddick (The Body Shop)
Marjorie Scardino (Pearson)
Lesley Smith (Dixons)
Kate Swann (Argos)
Barbara Wilding (Metropolitan Police)

# Foreword

## James Dyson

The best entrepreneurship involves, amongst other skills, getting passionate about a problem and solving it. Gains in profit, market share, and new markets are all significantly more likely to occur as a result of recent innovations. We have to realise how crucially important science, engineering and design are to this country. We need to inspire and empower scientists and engineers to be entrepreneurs – to develop new technology to solve problems.

So, as an employer, I am concerned that there are so few women who follow the engineering and manufacturing path. Despite our best efforts only 20 of the 350 engineers we employ at Dyson are women, and most of those have fathers who were themselves engineers and encouraged them from an early age.

Why is engineering so unappealing to women? The exceptions to the rule seem to indicate that it's the influence of the family and education that is directing young people, and especially young women, away from engineering and manufacturing. It seems that people are making a value judgement that these are inferior pursuits. Instead, we want our young people, and in particular our young women, to join a profession where, it is believed, status and respectability reside. And although no one likes to be accused of questioning the importance and validity of creativity and 'the creative industries', too few people automatically associate creativity with the tasks of engineering and manufacturing.

Yet designing and making things is an intelligent and a creative activity, and still people have a serious prejudice against it – they think working with your hands is not what clever people, and especially clever women, do.

Unfortunately our education system fails to produce a nation which either respects or gives priority to engineering and manufacturing. The majority of graduates want careers in the media. Engineering, sadly, is simply neither hip nor modern, and for most young people it offers no social or economic incentive. Well, I would like to assure them, men and women, that a career in this field is creative, and it is rewarding. At Dyson, not only are we now designing new products with new technologies that will come out within the next year, but we are also developing those that will replace them in 2002, 2003, 2004 and 2005. We employ scientists, engineers, designers, who all work together in purpose built, state of the art laboratories, researching and developing new technologies, because we cannot afford not to strive continuously for innovation. And we would like all employees to do things differently, almost just for the sake of it. This isn't some management trick – it constantly forces you to think through every move and it is fundamental to the way we develop new products. What it takes however, is passion.

The Americans have achieved this passion and ambition by creating prestigious and well-funded institutions such as the Massachusetts Institute of Technology. There are currently more than 4,000 companies that have been founded by MIT graduates and faculty. And as a result of the culture of innovation bred into their founders at the MIT, these companies are phenomenally successful. If they formed an independent nation, the revenues produced by these companies would make them the 24th largest economy in the world. Think of the contribution that a similarly motivated generation of engineers and business people could make to this country.

I believe in employing people, men and women, with thought processes that are unfettered and unsullied by previous experience. The country needs both men and women who are unencumbered by preconceptions, who can use this freedom to make a difference. I hope more of them will take up the challenge.

*[signature]*

# Introduction

As author, I have been sparked into writing this book because of the exciting strides forward being made by many women in Britain.

I also hope that you, the reader, can learn from the inspirational stories I have heard from those who are making it to the top. You will learn about how women are grabbing power in the City, in Westminster and in the world of law and the police. I am interested to know how far this trend can go.

More than this, I believe those who say that our commercial community, including media and retail, has not been making the best use of the talents of half of our population for decades.

This concerned me. I was curious to know why. I was interested to meet those who have smashed the so-called 'glass ceiling'. I am also minded to take notice of the extremely well-respected equal opportunities campaigner who told me about us reaching the 'springboard stage'.

As a City journalist, I remember being taken aback when I first found out that no British woman has ever been made Chief Executive of one of our top 100 companies. For, I am from the generation who were in their late teens and taking 'A' levels when Margaret Thatcher was becoming the country's first ever woman Prime Minister. As such, I had never worked in a culture that automatically assumed it was the men who always became boss. I believe I am open-minded enough to accept that women, even those younger than myself, can hold power over me.

In writing this book, I hope to show that men like my-self will increasingly have women bosses and leaders and that we will need to show we can accept and handle this situation.

Dare I say it, the sooner we do, companies, organisations, men, women, everybody, should benefit. Furthermore, if the causal link between the male-dominated business hier-archy and a 'macho', excessive, long-hours, work culture can be broken down, I believe we will all enjoy more bal-anced lives.

By reading about those I have interviewed, I hope you will enjoy getting to know women who are reaching the very top. I will be happy that you will get to know more about them before the population at large.

I have had my eyes opened by inspirational tales. These range from the young go-getter who put up with taking home less money than her nanny for many years on the route to success, to the business lady, who is now one of the richest in the country, but who initially felt she had to change her name to Steve in order to ever get off the ground. You will read about the young woman who had the unusual claim to fame of selling her husband to a rival team. You will hear why it is much more 'intellectually chal-lenging' to be at the top in business than it is at West-minster. And why women 'have to be twice as good, to be seen as half as good'.

My research also saw me transformed into a male 'fly-on-the-wall' as I was invited to find out how women are hitting back at 'Old Boys' Clubs' and developing a vibrant networking club culture of their own. I am grateful to High Tech Women and the other 'power networkers' for letting me in. I was only an honorary 'fly'. Not a very good one at that, dressed in a boring two-piece suit! But I did enjoy finding out at first hand what it feels like to be alone in an environment dominated by the other sex.

I was also fascinated to talk to one of our country's best ever female sports stars and learn about how she had to fight hard for years to be given an equal and deserved seat at Lords.

We are entering a fascinating period in the business world. Traditional routes to the top of our companies are breaking down. For instance, we are seeing how entrepreneurs of both sexes can 'get rich quick' in an age of e-commerce. We are also seeing how this technological revolution is creating a level playing field. A new meritocracy that does not favour one gender over the other. Also, opportunities are opening up like never before in areas like headhunting and 'image management'. Public relations professionals are having to be intelligent, skilled and ready to stand constant evaluation. In return, the 'fluffy PR girls' of the past are growing up to be communication pros with seats at the top table.

This book is about what it all means for our female adventure capitalists.

Will there be room at the very top of companies? Have women got what it takes to break the barriers that, up to now, have seen men dominate society?

Debate is raging at Westminster about whether or not our Parliament should be reformed to encourage more women to sit as our political leaders. I have enjoyed delving into the careers of the growing band of women who have made it to the top of Parliament. It is up to readers, and the electorate, to pass judgement on whether this trend can continue.

You will read about whether or not this country is catching up with the entrepreneurial culture that has been well established in the United States. And whether the trend seen across the pond of the fastest-growing businesses being led by entrepreneurial women is filtering through to Britain. Also, I wanted to find out why a string of US women have been preferred to home-grown talents to run top companies over here.

Above all, I wanted to find out what makes entrepreneurial women different.

Traditionally, business leaders have been male. Mostly, they have had 'entrepreneur's ear' in that they have been deaf to everyone and everything else, except an inner driving voice.

Surveys have shown that more and more women in this country are taking the plunge and heading their own enterprises. It is thought that entrepreneurial women are driven more by the aim of job-creation than the goal of wealth accumulation. This is something I applaud.

Furthermore, across all businesses, women are holding three times as many managerial positions than they did a decade ago. When it gets to seats in the boardroom, women are still under-represented. However, there has been progress. Ten years ago, only about one in fifty companies had women board directors. Today, about one in ten have women. This is also a trend I applaud and I believe the so-called 'feminine' skills have a valid place at the very top of the management tree. More than this, women's skills need to be tapped. The new knowledge-based economy will really value those who can hold teams together, rather than create divisions and hierarchies.

You may be set thinking about how you would improve your own company or organisation. With this in mind, I asked one of the country's leading venture capital firm directors what the purpose of a board, or top team, was. 'Find the right strategy, the right resources . . . and keep out of jail!' was the reply.

There was an element of tongue in cheek in the answer, but it was not a bad summary about how limited chairmen might have been in their thinking and aspirations in the past. The venture capitalist then told me: 'Companies have never changed the people on their boards frequently enough to fit circumstances.' The UK economy depends on using the talents of all its people. Individual companies will find women are becoming increasingly important customers and making more of the spending decisions. It is high time the make-up of boardrooms is changed to fit twenty-first century circumstances.

During the course of this book you will read about how several areas of business life have been more fertile grounds than others for women ambitious enough to be 'number one'.

Engineering has traditionally been a more barren area. But in James Dyson, this country has produced one of the most visionary and successful entrepreneurs in modern life. Of the characters I have interviewed, he is one I came away admiring the most. The kind of person, male or female, that I relate to. James Dyson has all the qualities that anyone wishing to come out on top 'against the odds' needs. And more besides. Recently, Dyson won a landmark court battle against Hoover in which he had to fight for years to prevent Hoover unfairly infringing patents on his revolutionary bagless vacuum cleaner. 'You have to be as dogged in solving the commercial problems you meet as you were in solving the creative challenge that turned your idea into reality in the first place', he says.

Dyson has the passion, even the obsession, needed to succeed. His story has many lessons in it for aspiring women and men who seek to make a difference. My jaw dropped when he told me he went through 5,127 proto-types before deciding his first Dyson was 'right'. Not widely known, but true, is the fact he suffered from meningitis while he was also battling to get his business off the ropes. Many entrepreneurs have him to thank for campaigning on their behalf. He is patriotic and it matters to him that the international big boys do not win with bully tactics. I could go on. . . . But, for the purposes of this book, and for our chances of future prosperity, I think we can pinpoint an important sentiment. . . . The concept of 'thinking differ-ently'. For women, men and everyone, it is time our leaders started thinking differently.

I am delighted he has penned his own thoughts in the Foreword, to add to mine.

# Author's Biography

As a journalist and writer Sam Parkhouse has won respect for his clear and entertainingly readable style. Also for his ability to make sense of even the most complex of subjects. He also has experience of interviewing and getting to know a host of very senior business entrepreneurs and politicians.

As a business, features and general reporter and a profile-writer he has a reputation for superb 'news sense'. Through his work, readers really get to know what drives the modern day 'gods and goddesses' and why they do what they do.

In his career he has written for national papers like the *Financial Times*, the *Daily Mail* and the *Evening Standard* and been city correspondent for the national news agency.

He comes from a family of writers, who have between them written a handful of Royal biographies and chronicled the life of one of Britain's most popular cabinet ministers. Father, Geoffrey, was a political editor at Westminster for 22 years and chaired the Parliamentary Lobby.

In his recent influential work *Big Banks & Small Businesses* Sam covered the often sour relationships between banks and the public and predicted shake-ups in the financial world.

# 1

# *Eve of a New Era*

## Martha Lane Fox

As the e-revolution sweeps Britain, Martha Lane Fox is its most public face.

Being young, female, intelligent and pretty gives her the ingredients to defy conventional routes to business success. But these ingredients alone are not sufficient to explain her meteoric rise to fame and wealth. After all, many models and actresses have been there before – some of them without the benefit of much intelligence.

For Martha is smart and has enormous drive. Smart in the sense that she latched on to the changing tide before everyone else. Smart also in the streetwise sense in that she recognises her feminine credentials and the way these, when allied to being very media friendly, can be used to benefit her business.

'If you have a dream, I believe you should do everything you possibly can to make it happen', says Martha. And anyone meeting her while she strives to develop lastminute.com is left in no doubt about how hard she works at it.

Knowing these factors about Martha takes us a long way towards putting a finger on why she has become such a household name, so quickly. Lady luck. And Martha does indeed agree that she has been lucky. Is this her most essential ingredient?

Go back a few years. There is the fascinating tale that reveals how much she owes to meeting her co-founder Brent Hoberman and his faith.

In a supreme irony, given the online booking concept that is the essence of her fame, Martha actually rejected his idea for lastminute.com by means of a long e-mail detailing exactly why she thought the plan wasn't a runner.

Martha had graduated from Oxford in 1994 and her first job was in a management consultancy. At this consultancy, called Spectrum, she first met her destiny. Not only was one of her earliest projects a presentation to BT called 'What is the Internet?', it was here, while working on a project for Carlton TV on its pay per view channels, she encountered Brent, a bubbly South African with infectious belief and just four years her senior. In a turnaround that has now gone down in e-legend, she had her eyes opened to the simplicity of the concept of a clearing house for late bookings on anything from holidays to gifts. And over Easter 1998 the pair put their business plan together.

Of course, Martha has also been lucky in a more general sense. Why she has risen so swiftly that she has even been called the fifth most influential woman in the country is down to an incredible sea-change in the business landscape. Revolutionary is an over-used word in hyping circles. But in the context of technology and online business it is not.

In just a handful of years, Internet screens have mush-roomed from being owned by a very small percentage of the population to being owned by one in five of us with no end of growth in sight.

This revolution offers prizes to its victors in the shape of incredible wealth at breakneck speed. In doing so, it tears up all previous wisdom on how to rate and value companies. Take Martha's. It was afforded a value of a mind-boggling £750 million at the height of the hype that surrounded its float in March 2000. Martha, with her 6.5 per cent stake, was instantly given a personal fortune of nearly £50 million in a company that had sales of just £34 million in 1999–2000. No matter that, for a fledgling company, it is making heavy losses. In its first six months as a plc, lastminute lost £17 million and, even by the end quarter of 2000, it was still £15 million in the red.

But the point is that lastminute and its dot com counterparts are new and unusual.

Lastminute is in a whirlwind involving attracting suppliers and customers at explosive rates. Lastminute.com, for instance had just one hundred suppliers at the start of 1999 and by the middle of 2000 this was climbing above 2,500. As acting as a kind of market-maker in spontaneity, her company does not really own anything. lastminute.com has just £35,000 worth of stocks at any one time, the equivalent of just half a day's trading.

Likewise customers, in the shape of those who registered as potential users of the site, ballooned to 2.9 million. However, the big challenge is converting potential customers into reality. Here lastminute.com does look exposed to the sceptics. During its first full year, lastminute admitted that only 156,000 had bought goods or services and so could be counted as customers in the conventional sense.

♀

Despite initial setbacks in public company life, lastminute. com nevertheless took strides forward in the year 2001.

Martha, after completing a multi-million pound takeover in France, claims lastminute.com has been 'catapulted into a different league'. Also, that hers 'is now Europe's biggest e-commerce business behind Amazon'.

In early 2001 another interesting corporate deal was signed. Under this, lastminute.com agreed to direct customers wishing to make bookings more than six weeks in advance of going on their holidays towards Thomas Cook. In return, Thomas Cook agreed to refer to lastminute.com its clients seeking theatre tickets and restaurant bookings.

Martha's pulling power saw the former Asda and Wal-Mart Europe supermarkets boss, Allan Leighton, attracted to become lastminute's non-executive chairman. Allan Leighton, according to Martha, has a reputation as a 'high-energy and very focused' retailer. Luring him: 'Is all part of our move to be considered a real retailer', she says. 'We knew instantly we met him we wanted to make it work', said Martha. Whether the chemistry and clashing of egos between the new chairman and the two entrepreneurial founders 'works' is obviously going to matter a great deal.

In what Martha likens to a cut throat 'Wild West' climate breaking through new frontiers in business, old preconceptions based on assets or debt ratios or how entrepreneurs arrived at where they are now, go out of the window. This means only entrepreneurs with ideas that capture the new age are handed out incredible millions by the financial markets. Lack of a track record or the gender of the entrepreneur matters less.

For those who work in such a revolutionary climate, there has been an equal upheaval in the ways of business. In an amusing twist amid the struggle between the old and new economies, lastminute.com started out in a tower block at the back of Dixons in Oxford St, Europe's biggest conventional shopping street. Within three months of its public float, lastminute had grown in staff numbers and needed to move, 'because everyone needed their own desk'.

'Everything at lastminute happens so fast', said Martha and half her team moved to brighter offices in Buckingham Gate but, because the company still couldn't afford to have everyone under the same roof, the customer services side was separated and looking for another location.

While Martha herself, as one might expect of someone of her blue-blooded background, dresses with taste and dresses on the smarter end of the smart casual scale, her staff don't look businesslike. A visitor arriving in a suit would feel uncomfortable when faced with banks of computer terminals staffed by young men and women, who if they dressed down any further would be ready for the bath.

But there you see another departure from 'old economy' companies. The vast majority of Martha's staff never deal face-to-face with anyone.

Martha has been hailed as the 'first lady of the Internet'. She and envy have not been far apart in the eyes of many people. Being the rich 'girl' and a 'winner', on paper, behind the lastminute.com float flop, while thousands suffered, makes this inevitable. To the 180,000 or so private investors who still are coming out in the red on the float, it is scant consolation that Martha is finding life tough.

♀

'It is all-consuming. Work is very, very, tough. The stakes have got higher now we are public', says Martha. 'There is no end in sight to the 14 hour days', the 27-year-old co-founder of lastminute adds.

'I spend 99.9 per cent of my time on spreading the word about lastminute.com, talking to the City and doing things like being available for the media. I also spend 99.9 per cent of my time developing the business and talking to suppliers, for this is a 200 per cent job', she says with a smile.

'I'm very flattered by all the attention being an Internet pioneer attracts. I do it because it is an amazing environment and I don't get out of bed just for the money. I rationalise the attention by saying we were one of the first companies to jump when the US Silicon Valley culture moved to the UK and yes, I recognise that being a young blonde does help.'

Martha says the millions she is worth, on paper, have not fuelled great spending frenzies. 'The only thing about my life that has changed is that I have no personal time. In the past I would arrive at parties early and bouncy. Now I arrive at midnight, grumpy and exhausted', she says.

During 2000–2001, the public was burnt in the float as lastminute slumped to a low of around 35p from its offer price of 380p, and the shares still languish at less than a quarter of their debut price. Insult was added to injury for the ordinary public as the 'grey market' share price for City institutions soared briefly to above 500p.

But Martha and her co-founder Brent Hoberman are still on the winning side. Martha's paper fortune may have dived from its peak of nearly £50 million, but her ground-breaking Internet travel and retail company has its £125 million worth of start-up funds safe in the bank. The pair of entrepreneurs say this buys enough time over the next three years until lastminute makes its first profit.

Meanwhile, Martha has gained the tag of our most famous businesswoman and is recognised as the most powerful face in the e-revolution. 'I'm so lucky to do what I've done. There is a definite upside. It is exciting and the work still makes me bounce out of bed.' She is still worth many millions for her part in an idea launched just two years ago and comfortably off with a £100,000 salary.

Martha says money is not what she is about. 'I did not set out to rule the world', she says. 'My family is absolutely the most important thing.'

In fact, Martha originally wanted to be a prison governor. And, surprising as it may seem, with the intoxication of all the attention still fresh, she does think about taking a back seat and she is already dreaming again of 'doing good'.

'I want to take what I have learned from all this and use it in a more socially responsible way.' She has written to inmates since she was a teenager. She is on the board of

'Retrieve' which campaigns in the USA on behalf of those prisoners on Death Row: 'I don't believe that you should be sentenced to death – whatever you have done', she says.

The socio-political left wing intellectual side of her nature may surprise those expecting her to be a flashy, young, product of the age when money conveys power. But many of her Westminster and Oxford educated generation are making a lot more as solicitors, or corporate financiers or whatever in the City. It would be wrong to say she is not ambitious. 'We are building a brand and we want to create the best website in Europe.' But this ambition is tainted as she recognises the lack of balance in her life. On a personal level this means she dreams about the day when she can get out of the office by early evening and see more of her friends. She hopes, 'one day I will have loads of children, maybe four, maybe a whole football team'.

Martha is the product of an aristocratic background. Directly descended from the Marquess of Anglesey and the Lane Fox estate agency founder, she went to one of the poshest public schools, Westminster, and Oxford. While studying history at Oxford she originally had a career in the prisons in mind. It was only through meeting last-minute's co-founder Brent Hoberman that she was persuaded on the road to business fame.

'I'm incredibly aware of serendipity in my life. I remember thinking that rather than follow the moral course, it is better to do something I enjoy and something I have more chance of being a success at', Martha says.

Friends from her days when she was one of just 30 or so sixth form girls at Westminster School remember her as bright, sweet and fairly quiet. Also as an irritating swotty type who became teacher's pet and got top marks no matter what she wrote. Her father, Robin Lane Fox is a don teaching ancient history at New College, Oxford, and also a gardening correspondent for the *Financial Times*. He divorced when Martha was 20 and her mother Louisa now lives in London. 'My father is a lot of things – an inspiration, very clever – but he's not very interested in money.' Martha remembers her parents being 'very pushy on academic training'.

At Magdalen studying history, Martha is recalled as a really nice, slightly earnest girl who was 'very together, if not exactly cool'. Even in university days there were signs of her singlemindedness, when aroused. For instance, when she lost out in a hall ballot to allocate rooms, she got really cross and wrote to college officials saying it was unfair and asking, without success, for a new ballot.

Martha is a stout proponent of so-called 'elite education'. 'It gave me a phenomenal amount of confidence. The confidence to fight the boys. My tutors constantly challenged me and I came out with the ability to think on my feet.' She again acknowledges that being a girl has its advantages when remembering how university tutors would give a much harder time of it to some male contemporaries when dissecting their tutorials. Also she recalls, with pleasure, how she was awarded the history prize at school and how this upset the boys.

It is the ingrained outlook of challenging and constantly re-appraising things that gives Martha the inclination to consider a life that does not involve being 'number one'. 'One of my roles is to be critical of myself as lastminute grows. The nuts and bolts of the business is in my blood. But I hope it will one day grow beyond me. We have gone from nothing to 250 staff in two years. Before long we could have 500. Skills of being a founder and skills of running a huge public company are very different. I look forward to taking a step back, though I think I will always be involved in my "baby"', Martha said.

♀

When talking about her company's service, she shows she has not entirely shrugged off her management consultancy background. Phrases like 'virtuous circles of conversion' trip off her tongue when talking about how lastminute converts airline's unsold inventories into tickets for customers. lastminute is 'an aspirational brand that has mainstream appeal'. They also offer 'a real-time yield management tool kit', by Martha's admission 'a hideous phrase', but nevertheless one that hints that lastminute will try and make money as a middle man and manipulate the prices upwards if there is too much demand for any specific holiday or hotel booking.

Like all successful consultants, Martha has customer service still firmly in her mind. We won't believe her when she claims there is little difference between her e-retailing business and traditional bricks and mortar retailers. After all, the whole point of the company is that it is offering something completely new and cool. 'We just happen to deliver through the Internet. But the same challenges face us all. The focus is on delivering service and value to our customers', she says. But, we will be happy to hear her talk the customer service talk.

She began her working life in 1994 as a 'fresh 21-year-old' in consultancy, 'looking at the impact of new technology and strategies for new areas of business'. Martha says the subject matter of this work provided a firm base to being an e-commerce entrepreneur. However, she worked in small teams then. 'Nothing ever really can prepare you fully for the demands, excitement and the total involvement of running your own company.'

Martha has her own mission statement for her company. She wants to: 'Encourage spontaneous, romantic and sometimes adventurous behaviour by helping our users to live their dreams at unbeatable prices'.

As the most well-known 'babe' in the e-commerce revolution, Martha says she feels 'very lonely' and says it is a 'terrible and awful situation' that so few women make it to the top of British business.

So how has the float flop affected her?

'It wasn't me at fault personally. I have never lived by watching what the media says about me. I was upset by the crappy and appalling service of our registrars IRG which meant a handful of shareholders didn't get certificates. I now see it was wrong to allocate people just 35 shares. It was foolish to assume that everyone would be a long-term investor.'

But the cool and cold business side of her nature is never far from view. 'It was Morgan Stanley's job to get the maximum money possible for us. In that sense we were lucky the float in March was just before the tech stock crash and not planned for a week later. . . . We were not to know that the day we went public, technology stock markets around the world would collapse. It was the ultimate last-minute irony', Martha said. This showed she has a ready sense of humour. But someone as bright as her, we know, deep down, must have been upset with advisers who misjudged the mood of the market.

'What I care much more about is my staff. No one has yet left to go to a rival, though a few have left because they were incompetent. It has been far more upsetting for me on the occasions when I have had to sack people', Martha said.

Her partner Brent says of the technology stock crash: 'It is disappointing for European e-commerce companies that are not now going to be given the opportunity to invest for growth'.

A couple of months after lastminute's public debut, Boo.com, a high-profile online sportswear retailer fronted by a Swedish model, went bust. Also, Clickmango.com, with famous actress Joanna Lumley on board as its public face, went under.

Does Boo.com's failure unnerve her? 'That was sad. Who knows how many will survive? It could be two, three or four. It's like the Wild West in this brave, new world. But comparing us to Boo just because we both have .com in our titles is silly. It is like comparing British Airways and British Telecom because they both have British in their names', Martha said.

'This is not an easy business to do, or to replicate', says Brent Hoberman. However, it was not long before others tried. British Airways and a consortium of ten European airlines including Air France and Lufthansa teamed up to form an online travel agency. Also, three of the largest hotel chains, Granada, Accor and Hilton launched a joint online hotel booking service. These moves are perceived to add competition to lastminute.com. Amidst this, lastminute reacted by broadening away from travel into gifts and restaurant bookings.

In any event, in summer 2000, lastminute.com did gain inclusion in the Techmark 100 index of leading UK technology stocks. 'It was great to be included. Techmark recognises the importance of technology stocks in the economy. The move means we are followed by a wider circle of fund managers', Martha said.

So has all the fame changed her? People who have worked at lastminute say she is always perfectly nice and a good boss. She obviously has the necessary touch to relate to a range of people. For instance by going round the office asking her staff what they thought about 'issues' before an appearance on 'Question Time' on television.

No doubt Martha is aware that being young and feminine can be an asset in the business world and it is said that her manner can sometimes be flirtatious. It is rumoured that Martha was nicknamed 'Fast Lane Foxy' at school, although she denies it.

As co-founder of lastminute.com Martha has been actively involved in all aspects of the business's development from securing new investment to recruiting senior staff to run the business in the UK and overseas. She has particular responsibility for the supplier relationships that drive the deals on the site, working with airlines, hotel chains, major entertainment promoters and restaurants. However, Brent Hoberman is chief executive of lastminute. He came up with the idea for the company because he says: 'I'm a compulsive procrastinator, I can't plan anything'. He is happy to let Martha be the public face because 'She is prettier than me and she is a good ambassador for the Internet. It makes people realise it is not just run by geeks eating cold pizza'.

During the year 2000, the pair of them kept the ball rolling with new dimensions for their company.

They launched a WAP mobile-phone service in a deal with the biggest telecoms companies in France and Germany to allow customers to book things on the move. They also had to completely overhaul their computer website and systems, within six months of lastminute's public debut. 'A huge project. We rebuilt the back end of the architecture, though we were mindful of not doing anything that put at risk customer satisfaction', Martha said.

Furthermore, lastminute.com also made its first big acquisition deal when it bought French rival Degriftour for £59 million. Degriftour had the advantage of being profitable and already running half of the French online travel market. Martha and her partner Hoberman claimed the deal would help them shorten the period until their own business moved into the black.

Formerly head of network development at Carlton Digital Channels, Martha was in that job responsible for generating and analysing new channel and interactive concepts. Her role saw her involved in negotiating with UK and international distribution partners to develop the Carlton brand overseas.

Prior to Carlton, Martha worked for three years as an Associate at Spectrum Strategy Consultants where she specialised in 'pay television' and managed teams in both the UK and Asia. These early days were useful in teaching the value of brands. Perhaps, this is why Martha was not deterred when she learned that a Sardinian businessman had already registered 'lastminute' as a name. She was adamant her company had to be called by that name and she and Brent bought the name for 'a few thousand pounds'. 'The brand is vital. It has quite a sexy image. We're not trying to be a big computer company; we're about empowering the consumer', revealed Martha as lastminute.com was planning its float.

Should her venture really 'take off', Martha Lane Fox herself will go down as a brand name signifying the new ways of doing business. In the next chapter, we explore the way other women entrepreneurs are rising in the new age.

# 2

# *Shifting Sands*

When technology became the 'sexy' industry, it opened doors in business to a whole new wave of women.

In the late 1990s, women and men with their own Internet ideas found themselves being courted by bankers with wads of money to throw into new ventures. As we have seen, this gave young female entrepreneurs like Martha Lane Fox, riches and a very high profile, very quickly. Dozens of other young women have been able to grab the coat tails of the Internet boom.

We shall look at a variety of go-getting women and their ideas later. Also, at how whole new types of industry sector, like headhunting, have popped up in the world and taken women to the top.

First, the story of a publicly-quoted software company, FI Group, and the story of the women behind its success, provides a fascinating insight into just how things are changing.

Hilary Cropper, as FI Group's chief executive, won the title of Britain's highest paid woman in 1999 when she made a staggering £17.4 million.

♀

This remarkable pay package has been possible because of her own skills, but in truth, has its roots in the remarkable tale of FI's founder, Dame 'Steve' Stephanie Shirley.

She originally came to Britain aged five as a refugee from the Nazis. 'I came over on a Kindertransport in 1939 with my sister with luggage labels tied around our necks', Dame Shirley recalls.

Then in 1962, Shirley founded her own computer services firm called Flexible Information at the age of 28 in reaction to what she found to be an impossible situation of combining career and family at the time, after working at the Post Office as a teenager. Stephanie's concept was based on the need to offer women flexible hours. Unfortunately, she realised that in the early 1960s it was a male-dominated industry and she felt she had to take the radical step of adapting her name to be called 'Steve' to get on.

By making the most of difficult childhood circumstances and by having a determination to learn from adversity, Stephanie Shirley has succeeded.

Talking about that first journey to Britain she says: 'In those circumstances, you learn very quickly that you have to make things happen rather than letting them happen to you.'

'It certainly makes you determined never to be poor again – and when I say poor, I mean fainting with hunger poor. The other thing is that you never expect tomorrow to be the same as today, which gives you a resilience and an ability to cope with change. Even today I'm still looking all the time for new ways to do things.'

Stephanie's son died through autism at the age of 35 and she has used millions of pounds to fund an autism charity. Even in the dark days at home with her son she saw a way of finding inspiration for work. 'In a way, work was an antidote to the terrible problems at home. It was exciting and different and you could solve the problems at work.'

Dame Stephanie is now retired with the title of life president and she probably reflects wistfully at how much easier it is today, but she has been rewarded by seeing her stake in FI grow to be worth more than £135 million.

Meanwhile, Hilary Cropper, 59, heads a group of women at FI who are all worth millions.

Cropper started in computing after her 'A' Levels with Associated Electrical Industries. During the 1970s she took a career break to bring up a family of three before joining ICL in 1976 and eventually rising to become the most senior female.

In 1985, she was headhunted to lead FI Group at a stage in the company's life when it still had a modest turnover of £8 million. Cropper switched the emphasis away from providing ad hoc firefighting on software glitches to winning huge, all-embracing consultancy contracts with top blue-chips like Tesco and banks like the Royal Bank of Scotland. In 1991 Cropper also masterminded a staff share ownership scheme of FI and in the few years after the company floated in 1996 the share price grew tenfold. Cropper's own personal fortune is above £60 million, while her commercial director at FI, Lyn Barrat and chief operating officer Jo Connell are also both paper millionaires.

And in the new climate in Britain, female entrepreneurs are beginning to oust those relying on inherited wealth in the list of the country's richest women.

Nikki Beckett, 39, with around £90 million, is among the 400 most wealthy people in the country. The former IBM executive is now chief executive of her own software company, NSB Retail Systems, which provides computer systems for High Street stores and which became quoted on the stockmarket in 1997. She has helped to transform a tiny start-up into a transatlantic business with 1,600 staff that has soared in value since its early days over five years ago to be worth £640 million.

She takes home a salary package and dividends of £238,000 a year. Beckett, who has her own family, says her secret is having a husband Geoff who agreed to become a house-husband and look after their two children most of the time.

Beckett tries to tackle the contradictory goals of being a perfect mother and a perfect businesswoman by dividing time between business and home. 'I am NSB 100 per cent of the time. I take weekends devoted completely to my sons, but I have to accept I cannot be perfect at everything.'

She also relates how making money drives her on. 'I have probably got more than I could ever spend. But it is all part of the milestones I set myself. It is all a measure of my success', she says.

Nikki Beckett's attitude to money is interesting. It tells us something about the motivations of top entrepreneurs. 'I'm much more interested in how I am going to make the next £100 million than in how I spend the £100 million that I have already made. I see money as a scorecard and that is why I count it', she revealed in a *Daily Mail* interview.

The entrepreneur also recognises how her gender has brought advantages. 'It is definitely easier being a woman. Many people agree to see you out of curiosity and you can then exploit the opportunity', she said.

The amazing success of the new computer games industry has been the making of Jane Cavanagh. She began her games company SCI Entertainment in 1988 and it joined the stock market in 1996 and 43-year-old Jane has shares which make her worth £32 million.

Julie Meyer is a woman who was part of the founding team of First Tuesday, a matchmaking club for techno-entrepreneurs seeking start-up funds. She is not untypical in seeing her idea pay off at incredible speed in the new economy. First Tuesday came into being following a cocktail party in October 1998 which set the idea in motion for a club that meets on the first Tuesday of every month and throws together people with Internet ideas and bankers with money, in the same room. It is like a type of cattle-market for techno-entrepreneurs. The club's founders benefit by taking 2 per cent of anything raised for deals. And despite the techno stock crash, First Tuesday was itself bought in 2000 for £34 million by an Israeli investment firm wishing to expand the concept in the USA and Julie Meyer moved on to her next business, Ariadne Capital.

The new, buzzy, high tech economy also gave former city worker Hazel Moore the idea for an entrepreneurial match-making service using the web itself.

FirstStage Capital is the first service in the UK focused on technology start-ups that uses the Internet to deliver investment opportunities to its network of private investors and venture capitalists.

FirstStage was founded in November 1999 by Hazel Moore and her husband Jason Purcell. Hazel Moore, chairman and co-founder is, like Jason, a Chartered Financial Analyst and was previously Head of Research for the Hong Kong equity research department of Indosuez–WI Carr Securities. Jason was previously a City analyst with UBS and Merrill Lynch and the founders are active business angels themselves. Their website is therefore designed to suit the needs of investors as well as those of entrepreneurs. These go-getters will be technology start-ups seeking first stage funding of between £50,000 and £1 million.

In 1997 Hazel quit investment banking, and she set up the business with the help of money made during her City career. Hazel's business allows investors to specify their areas of interest, and browse through previously screened summaries of business plans that fit in with their own personal criteria. The focus is solely on seedcorn capital, which might come from one individual or from a syndicate, or from venture capitalists.

Hazel says about the more traditional routes available for entrepreneurs: 'It is very ad hoc and inefficient at the moment and difficult if you don't meet the venture capitalists' radar screens.'

First Stage was launched just months after the pair had their first baby. 'It was a very hard balance to strike. When you are setting up a company it is manic anyway', said Hazel. In the short life of her new company she found that: 'If there are women techno-entrepreneurs, it tends to be in certain well defined areas – companies which cater to the arts, special interest sites, or in marketing positions. Women who have been successful tend to be disproportionately well known like Martha Lane Fox. However on the positive side these women are now role models, and the Internet is not seen as so much of a technical geeky area. This will probably do a lot to encourage women to start up their own businesses.'

Hazel, when asked whether aptitudes vary between the sexes in technology said: 'I have not come across any good reason as far as my own experiences are concerned which would point up a reason for a disparity between the genders. It's not like in the City where glass ceilings, exclusion from male banter and support networks are still a reality for many women.'

'All I can say is that I hope and believe that the barriers to entry, whether real or perceived, to women in the new economy will be lowered with Internet speed', First Stage's Hazel said.

Before the bubble burst in technology stocks, the so-called 'business-to-consumer' market was a fertile ground for entrepreneurs. As Internet use for web sites took off in popularity from the 'backwater status' of use by just 5 per cent of the population in 1996 to more than 21 per cent in 2000, women made up an increasingly greater percentage of customers.

Since 1999, this has in turn fuelled a new market of a rash of websites aimed at women. There are three which attracted big-name backing from the media industry, with *Daily Mail* publisher Associated Newspapers getting behind Charlotte.com, the Hollinger Group and Boots backing Handbag.com and Freeserve plc funding iCircle.

A huge element in the output of these websites reflects what is already available on the shelves in women's magazines but this does not disguise the opportunities that have been opened up.

Hilary Burden, 38, spearheaded IPC's new women's website, Beme.com, and says: 'the beauty of the Internet is that a lot of male prejudices don't exist'. Narda Shirley, 33, is MD of her own firm Gnash Communications and she says: 'The nice thing about the Internet is that, because it is so new, it's a total meritocracy. It is not old enough to be dominated by men and there is no glass ceiling and it's rare that women are pushed to the front so quickly.'

As Internet usage took hold, even the old-established businesses were forced to take note and get involved. Even the blue-chip auction houses Sotheby's and Christies, felt the need to embrace the new challenges of the new ways to do business. Penny Jerram worked on the development of Sotheby's auction website, which she described as a means to offload the bottom end of the art market away from the traditional auction room, before she became an entrepreneur in her own right as the launch MD of Defining Edge, her firm which acts as a middle-man in home furnishing between small-scale producers and the bigger stores.

Elinor Chadwick, at 28, started her career as a mergers and acquisitions specialist at the niche City firm, Catalyst, before also seizing an opportunity in the way the art market was moving with the times. Elinor founded her Premierfind.com in autumn 1999 to provide back-up services for art and antique dealers. 'If anything it is a huge advantage being a woman. It opens a lot of doors. But I find it is a generational thing. People who are 20 years older than me comment on my being a woman while to those of my own age it is not an issue', Elinor says about the new climate.

Under the old regime, personnel, and the more grandiose-sounding cousin that came from the USA, human resources, provided two arenas where women did reach near the top of companies. Often there would be a woman personnel director but that title alone did not come with a seat on the main board.

This is changing with the new age in business. With the service sector making up a dominant portion of the UK economy comes the realisation that people are a company's most important asset. It is natural that the director in charge of this should have status at group board level to reflect this. To take one example, Stephanie Monk as human resources director at the Granada media and leisure group, was a crucial figure following Granada's £34 billion takeover of the Forte hotel chain in 1996. She also has close links with 'New Labour' and was an expert adviser on the new minimum wage legislation in 1998. For her Granada job, Monk took home a package worth £564,000 in salary and share options last year.

Barbara Ward owes her fortune of around £90 million to the happy coincidence of combining a personnel career and being in the software revolution. Ward joined the London-based group CMG software in 1965, became a director twelve years later and now heads personnel at CMG and became a beneficiary as it has been a runaway stockmarket success since 1995.

The new power-wielding profession of headhunting also propels many women well into the club of Britain's most well-paid professionals. Gillian Carrick, now 57, switched track nearly twenty years ago from a lighting company to join headhunter Goddard Kay Rogers. Today, she leads the firm and has a reputation as the leading media headhunter after finding a new chief executive for Capital Radio and helping find bosses for the Arts Council and Channel Four.

The headhunting profession has seen women like Anna Mann grow in stature alongside the growth in the industry itself and she went on to head Whitehead Mann.

The industry is attractive to female executives who seek a degree of flexibility in their work and has attracted women from other professions. To name but two, former

*Times* journalist Carol Leonard, now runs Leonard Hull International, the firm that also attracted Ffion Hague, the wife of Tory Leader, William Hague.

People and administration skills provide an obvious route to top board positions. And in the case of Yve Newbold the two combined to make her known as 'the most powerful woman in British industry' in one life and one of the most influential headhunters in her next. Yve Newbold won the first tag as company secretary at Hanson plc in the decades when Lord Hanson's group built itself into being one of the top industrial conglomerates in the world. Being company secretary at a time when so many multi-billion pound takeover deals were being hatched by Hanson gave her a central role in accelerating the pace of change in the business landscape and this experience was backed up by a directorship at British Telecom.

She is now chair of the business campaign, the Ethical Trading Initiative. Also, as she was a senior partner at headhunter Heidrich & Struggles she, uniquely, has first hand personal experience of the shifting sands of business life for women. In the 1970s at Hanson she was almost alone at the top, but now she works in a climate where breakthroughs are becoming common.

'In the past many of us had to act as surrogate men to be heard. But I detect a new mood about women in the boardroom. We have our own female qualities and we do not have to be ashamed of them', said Yve. These qualities include a better ability to understand the human heart through child-rearing, she claims.

About the prospects for women she says there has not been the critical mass of women at top level to draw from, but this at least forces a search for young female talent, which is a good thing. 'Women have to be serious to overcome the disadvantages of being young and female. They need to develop techniques for being heard, resilience, and learn not to be put off by rejection', she advises.

Yve Newbold is also an authority on how men in business use networking and charity roles to help further their careers. In a later chapter we shall see how women are increasingly 'clubbing with the men' and how this trend is also a growing force in the new business age.

# 3

# *Shaking the Tree*

## Anita Roddick

Anita Roddick is the world's most famous business woman. Her Body Shop group has spread to 50 countries from humble beginnings on the Sussex coast. She is also world famous as a 'green' campaigner. As such, her influence over the past 25 years means that Anita has become much more than a woman who has reached the top in business. Anita Roddick is a role-model for all successful women. An icon whose power stretches way beyond power that any riches from her business could bring.

The Body Shop's story is one that is fascinating to relate as it reaches its 'silver jubilee'. Then, for the purposes of my book, we shall be interested in what inspires and drives Anita Roddick and what lessons can be drawn for those women who also seek power and influence.

Anita says: 'Isn't it amazing how much can change in 25 years? I think back to 1975 for a moment. I was running a small restaurant in Littlehampton and wonderfully naive. There was no Internet, no palm pilots and there were just three TV channels. There even used to be a few village shops in those days!'

♀

Anita began by opening her first shop in Brighton with the help of a £4,000 loan from a local garage owner friend. Her drive then was simply to provide 'an honourable livelihood' for herself and her two daughters while her husband Gordon Roddick was away trekking between Buenos Aires and New York on horseback.

'The notion of me having to rely on Gordon for money makes me gag thinking about it', Anita once said long after the pair had successfully built Body Shop into an international business. Anita's share of Body Shop was worth £100 million and indeed she will never be short of money with annual income and dividends topping £1 million.

The ingredients of success for the Body Shop were drawn from Anita's own outlook and experiences. She trained as a teacher of English and History and this provided a base for the communications skills that were to be so important in making Anita what she is today. Also, the death of her father, when she was just ten, meant she was thrust into helping her mum run the family café business. 'I grew up with this notion that life wasn't any more complicated than love and work', Anita recalls.

Anita says travelling has always been part of her life. Kibbutz life in Israel as a student and living closely with the 'natives' in far flung places like Tahiti, Australia, Madagascar, the New Hebrides and many more are all experiences she distilled into the Body Shop philosophy and products. She felt conventional business environments alienated humanity and from day one rejected the hype and packaging excesses of the cosmetics industry. The idea of painting the shop walls green came from simply having to 'cover up the damp' in her cash-strapped beginnings and the idea of selling things in different-sized bottles came simply because she 'needed to fill the shelves'.

♀

As a woman in charge of a major cosmetics retailer Anita Roddick may have had a useful empathy with her main customers. 'Sensuality . . . it is the stuff of life', she has said, although she also once claimed her own personal use of make-up ends with moisturising her skin.

She believes values are every bit as important as profits and she has used the Body Shop as a platform to promote human rights, animal protection and environmental issues. It may be a happy coincidence that products sourced from people she really believes in, really seem to work and took off with western consumers. Like the Brazil Nut conditioner that really is good for dry hair and is sourced from Amazonian Indian community collectives.

What is not in doubt is that Anita Roddick's business and the green and environmental revolution went hand-in-hand. She certainly influenced a change in thinking. And for two decades the Body Shop rode high on the growing enthusiasm for green ideas.

Body Shop started expanding overseas in 1978. By 1984 it had joined the stock market. In 1986 its first headline-grabbing campaign, to 'Save the Whale' in partnership with Greenpeace, was running and helped in turn to fuel interest in the business. A couple of years later Body Shop opened in the USA. In retrospect this was the biggest move in Anita's business career and one that meant her store was on the way to growing to more than 1,500 across the globe. But it was part of an over-expansion that eventually led to Body Shop's profits downfall.

Meanwhile, Body Shop and Anita continued to make headlines with campaigns to save rain forests, by campaigning against animal testing, by campaigning generally to save us. Also Body Shop broke new ground by becoming the first leading company to decide for itself to issue environmental and social audits.

In the late 1980s, Body Shop was a darling in the eyes of the City and its value climbed to be worth more than £350 million. Had this love affair continued, Anita Roddick could well have become Britain's first female chief executive of a FTSE company.

But, she never shared this affection with the financial community.

When Body Shop was at its peak in 1987, it was nominated by the CBI as Company of the Year. Anita, in her forthright manner, referred in her acceptance speech to City folk as 'Those pin-striped dinosaurs in Throgmorton Street'.

Even when Body Shop was announcing results, Anita Roddick would often be conspicuous by her absence, travelling abroad. 'Finance bored the pants off me', she said. 'The so-called bottom line isn't actually the bottom line at all. And to me one of the most inspiring things over the past 25 years has been realising just how fundamental that message is. If there is a bottom line at all, for life as much as business, the bottom line is soil, and it's society, and it's also soul', she says.

It was left to Gordon Roddick, chairman, to explain things to the City and the press.

This attitude of not being 'available' to those who matter may have stored up resentment. Her own personal assistant told me; 'She is incredibly busy. Sometimes I find it impossible to get to see her, and I work in the next door office!'

In any event, in the early 1990s competitors in the USA grew and in Britain sales came under pressure as chains like Boots and the large supermarkets also began to sell their own ranges of natural cosmetics.

Anita has been known for her free-thinking. In her recent book *Business as Unusual* she openly refers to herself as being 'ballsy and non-conformist'. She is also quick to put her hand up to mistakes. Talking about dreadful over-expansion in the USA she says: 'The fact is, we just got everything wrong'.

Overall sales growth stalled and by the end of the 1990s the Body Shop share price had hit an all-time low of 80p, a new outside chief executive had come in and the company spent £21 million in restructuring costs to try and turn its fortunes around. The outsider, new chief executive Patrick Gournay did, however, promise not to tamper with the 'green and ethical' image. 'I am not an activist, but I realise this is not just an average cosmetics company, it is something unique', he said in 1998. Meanwhile, Body Shop has experimented in a home-selling programme, called Body Shop Direct, which runs in a similar way as the infamous Tupperware parties.

♀

There is no doubt that Gordon has been an important element in the Roddick team. 'Running a company is rather like a marriage. When it's going well, it's fantastic. When it's not, it's absolutely miserable', says Anita. 'Gordon does all the rubbish I can't do. In some ways he is more entrepreneurial than I am. He is always on the move, but he likes to come home', Anita once said in a *Mail on Sunday* interview.

For his part, Gordon has tried to put into context Anita's decision to hand over to a new boss. He says Anita's title of chief executive had always been a bit of a misnomer: 'She has been the creative impulse behind the business and that is what she will continue to be'.

Anita has also had to come to terms with the 'shock and total deflation' of her husband having an affair in 1999–2000. The affair, with a woman 20 years younger, is apparently over and Anita says: 'We ended up being kinder and much more aware of what nearly disappeared down the chute.'

Anita Roddick once said about herself and her husband partner Gordon: 'We're quite unemployable, extremely self-motivated, we hate hierarchy, we love a collegiate sense of informality, we are quite crazy in a way, so speedy, so fast, in such a hurry.' But Roddick, now 58, also recognises the dilemma she faced as a founder–entrepreneur when the company got too big. Due to the City pressure for change and partly due to her own desires to change, Anita took a step back from the helm of Body Shop. She is now just co-chairman, though the Roddicks do still have shares worth £63 million. Also Anita has been looking at new ventures, including involvement with the Ben & Jerry's ice cream business, involvement in a 'Green publishing' venture with Thorsons and taking a stake in the Hotel du Vin hotels chain. 'There are so many other things I want to do, like set up a publishing company. In your twenties, you want to feather your nest and know who you are going to marry. In your forties and onwards, you want to be surrounded by all the people you love, so you eliminate all the rubbish in your life', Anita says about how her life priorities have changed.

So, what does Anita's story tell us about the climate for top women in the business world?

I asked her about some of the things that readers would like to know about.

*Q: What do you actually believe about corporate life and women? For example, would this country be better if women gained equal power in the boardrooms? Is it the case that any woman who has been near the top has in fact done so by changing herself, by being a man?*

[Anita Roddick says:]

*A:* The image of women changing is a wretched misconception that lingers unlovingly on. These misconceptions of women's abilities endure because of the way we've been conditioned to believe in opposites: mind versus body; reason versus emotion; power versus partnership.

I feel the country would be better off if there was more power shared with women simply because, in the end, it's more natural. It's natural for women to want to share common practices. We want to act as if everything we do matters. It's this awareness that is at the root of the innate radicalism of women – and women's radicalism, unlike men's, tends to hold, as they age.

*Q: Has it ever been a hindrance being a woman in the business world?*

*A:* The major hindrance attached to my gender came in the form of an unhelpful bank manager very early on in the life of The Body Shop. Apart from that, there have been the inevitable jibes over the years that no journalist would think of directing at a male, but those kinds of challenges only confirmed me in my convictions.

*Q: Has it been an advantage being a woman?*

*A:* My mother always told me that a woman re-invents herself in her 50s. That's one advantage to being a woman.

[However, Anita has held her hands up and admitted that she was a less than perfect mother.]

For me, as a mother, time was always my enemy. I wasn't always there for the children. Home and hearth is not something I was good at.

For Anita, this once meant she did not have her antennae up for detecting a period of unhappiness for her eldest daughter, Justine, who responded by faking appendicitis.

'I feel I can be a better grandmother than a mother in a way', though being grandmother in itself is a 'crossroads' and the more high-voltage and high profile a woman in her youth the more difficult it can be to come to terms with middle age, she has said.

♀

Q: *Are there areas where women's skills are better for business?*

A: I know the debate rages on, but I believe there is a woman's way of doing business. Research from the USA suggests women managers are effective social initiators. They anticipate problems and possible solutions. Women build alliances, bring people together and most importantly, they develop networks.

Their biggest strength is communication, and that has been one of the things I'm most proud of with the success of The Body Shop. I can only see fame as a means to an end – it's a way to make messages heard.

Q: *How do you personally feel about your fame? i.e. are you proud and have you achieved changes in the status of women as a result of your fame? Would you like to see more?*

A: I would hope one of those messages is the empowerment of women, but for me, that came about by going in the opposite direction to everyone else.

The hierarchies founded on male authority remain unchanged, strengthened even by the juggernaut march of the multinationals. You have the professions controlled by men. Women have limited access to men's social networks. The moral of the story is: do your own thing. Women are brilliant entrepreneurs and grass roots activists. That's where the future lies!

Q: *What is your emotional attachment to Body Shop like? How are you coping with the changing management?*

*A:* It's an inevitable analogy – The Body Shop is my baby and the umbilical attachment will always be there. At the same time, the company had to reinvent itself to meet the future and that meant a new kind of input. I've been able to focus on what I enjoy and do best, acting as a creative greenhouse.

*Q: What other business ventures are in the pipeline?*

*A:* I'm working on setting up a publishing imprint with Thorson's Books, which will pursue environmental ideas independent of The Body Shop.

*Q: In your opinion, how far can the current green campaigns go to shake up the business world?*
*Will environmental reports, alternative fuels etc. make fundamental changes?*

*A:* I believe the wild card in big business now is vigilante consumerism. Consumer pressure is going to force fundamental changes, and obviously environmental concerns are fundamental to those changes. We shouldn't be compromising the future for the present's short-term needs.

*Q: From your perspective, what has Body Shop achieved in changing business thinking?*

*A:* The Body Shop was a pioneer in such thinking. We helped change the language of business, we proved by example that a company can generate profits while staying true to its principles, and at the very least, we compelled the cosmetics industry to assess its attitude to animal testing.

♀

So, what is it that keeps someone as well known and well off as Anita Roddick going and what things inspire her to keep putting her head above the parapet?

Anita has, in her own words, lived through 'a quarter of a century of insanity – from nutrasweet to the neutron bomb, from Greenham Common to gigabytes'.

Although well into her 50s, Anita has not lost any of her famed energy and this even manifested itself by being in the front line of a riot at a World Trade summit in Washington. 'I have to admit I got another insight about the so-called bottom line facing the police line in Seattle – a rather different kind of line in fact. In fact, I'm probably one of the very few international business people who can put their hands on their heart and say, they were tear-gassed at an international conference of the World Trade Organisation. Who knows, maybe it would have done some of the others some good', Anita said with tongue in cheek.

'And although I've been as outspoken as I dared over the past decade and more about the way the world trade and money system was set up to give as little attention as possible to soil, soul or society, Seattle was still a kind of watershed for me', she reflected. 'It taught me a number of things. It taught me that when men dressed in black body armour and wearing helmets bear down on you, it's usually best to run for it. It taught me that, however much companies like The Body Shop might develop a new kind of business – there was and is a real danger that the new trading system could undermine all the efforts and advances any of us made in the past quarter of a century. And it gave me another insight into the danger of narrow, inhuman and profit-and-loss style bottom lines. That, if it is entirely unregulated, business can and does become criminal', she says.

Anita also reveals how she continues to think differently from the typical business tycoon: 'I know as unemotional business people we are supposed to regard these lapses from grace in a completely objective, chilly and bloodless way. But I can't. I take it personally', she said. 'I take personally the babies I've held mutated by chemicals, or genetically handicapped by toxic wastes dumped in local streams. The more I travel, the more personal it seems', she added.

♀

However, Anita personally does see evidence of things changing for the better.

'And yet, and yet. Seattle was hopeful too. Between 40,000 and 60,000 people took part in the protests there. They included human rights activists, labour activists, indigenous people, people of faith, environmentalists, steelworkers and farmers. There were mums and dads, children, grandmothers and grandfathers.'

Also, Anita is pleased she has played a part in encouraging the investment community to be more proactive in fighting 'green' causes. She points to a new breed of so-called 'vigilante consumers'. 'All over the world, there are people who invest ethically, who refuse to buy from companies with poor records on the environment or human rights – what Faith Popcorn calls "vigilante consumers" – who are forcing this moral message on to the corporate agenda, whether they like it or not. Vigilante consumers are busily investing in companies with the right ethical profile – £2.5 billion is ethically invested in the UK alone – and they are shunning their unethical rivals. They are buying shares in a company and then turning up and hijacking the annual general meeting. No company can afford to ignore them. That inspires me', explained Anita.

Anita is also inspired by the human spirit and by human creativity. What she calls 'the astonishing ability of human beings to survive and keep hoping and bring up children – and the amazing ability people have to come up with simple creative solutions'.

One of the most powerful signs of human ingenuity is the rise of non-governmental organisations. What was once a small band of charities raising money to help the occasional person a little out of poverty, has grown into the vastly influential sector of the world. There are now about 26,000 international NGOs – four times as many as there were a decade ago. They are powerful at international level, but locally small NGOs are providing people with the ability to fight back. And giving at least the potential of a voice to some of those who are currently sidelined, muzzled and disempowered. 'And that inspires me too', she says.

They are taking on child labour and the right to education – and making a real difference to people's lives in some of the most difficult and challenging situations you can imagine. They are part of a global army of people delivering positive change, building community trade, raising hell at corporate AGMs, 'vigilante consumers' hitting back at the corporates that are undermining people's lives. They are all ordinary people with creative solutions. 'It's the brightest sign on the horizon for the world', thinks Anita.

'When I get down, as I do occasionally, about the future of the world – then thinking of this great life-enhancing creativity, and these ordinary people who display it, keeps me hopeful. It reminds me again that small isn't just beautiful. It's also creative and it's optimistic and it's the future', said Anita.

Anita says: 'At 58, I have reached an age where I think I did the best I could'.

# 4

# *In the Shop Window*

If you asked a member of the public to list top women in business, the chances are they would start with Anita Roddick. By founding the Body Shop and by her leading role in the 'green crusade' she is a household name.

But, go back to the original question – Women in business? The point is that Anita comes from retailing. Her Body Shop empire has contracted, and in the context of the economy it is not as influential as businesses in many other areas.

There are great barren areas of industry where women have barely stepped on to the ladder to the top. But retailing is one world where women have succeeded.

The fashion industry has spawned top names like Karen Millen, the clothing maker who heads her own name stores chain. And also Stella McCartney, the daughter of ex-Beatle Paul, who was promoted to run Chloe while only in her mid-20s before moving on to Gucci in 2001.

Rosemary Thorne became finance director of Sainsbury's at a time when it was still Britain's biggest supermarket group. When she was in this high position, she found that being a lone woman at the top can be difficult. Rosemary remembers times while on the board at Sainsbury when the men would in fact fix the real decisions in discussions 'in the men's loo' after formal gatherings in the boardroom had split up.

For a long while, Thorne was talked of as a candidate to become the UK's first women chief executive of a FTSE company, but a combination of Sainsbury's slump in fortunes and her own lack of the required personality to be a leader saw her slip. Thorne, 48, quit Sainsbury's in 1999 and is now finance director of Bradford & Bingley.

But women still keep coming through as success stories in the retail world.

Belinda Earl, at 38, took many people's breath away when she was made the new chief executive of one of Britain's favourite department store groups, Debenhams plc. When Earl hit the top in summer 2000, it came after a rapid rise up the ranks in a 15-year career at the stores group.

Her appointment is refreshing because, not only is she a woman and one of the youngest chief executives among the leading plcs, she appears to have an enlightened attitude to the pressures of work. The idea of 'being the first in to work and last out and the macho work ethic is a load of crap. No one is going to get "brownie points" for sitting at their desks well into the night and working in an inefficient way', she says.

Belinda Earl had retailing in her blood and grew up with an understanding of the 'consumer world' as her family owned a photography shop and an opticians in her home town of Plymouth.

She chose an Economics and Business degree to gain the necessary understanding of finance to make it in commerce. She shied away from chartered accountancy because she craved 'more interaction with people, more excitement'. She started out in retail at Harrods, but decided to leave because her career was being blocked 'by having to wait to fill dead men's shoes'. In the mid-1980s she was a protégé of previous Debenhams Group boss, Terry Green. By 1993, Earl had been promoted to the main board as Trading Director. In the late 1990s, she teamed up Debenhams with fashion designer Jasper Conran and he says of her that she has qualities of being 'firm, straightforward, she is not a pushover, but she is fair'. Joanna Lane-Jones, Corporate Communications Director, has worked closely with Belinda Earl at Debenhams. 'She is very focused, but also very easy to work with', she says.

'I want to use my position as chief executive to take Debenhams into the next century. This means placing extra emphasis on customer choice and trying to make sure Debenhams stores are available as widely as possible', says Earl. Her immediate plans are to extend the so-called 'personal shoppers', who latch on to customers and offer one-to-one shopping advice, to more of Debenhams' 100 stores. Also, to introduce 'Gold Card Lounges', with relaxation areas, for high-spending customers.

Belinda Earl would appear to be a star to watch for the future. Meanwhile, the country's best-known newsagent and bookseller, WHSmith, has a woman retail star with a long track-record already: Beverley Hodson.

♀

If you were looking for the most successful and powerful woman in business in the UK at the moment, Beverley Hodson is a person to watch. Her story tells us how she has used her passion for shopping to get to the top.

Beverley Hodson is managing director in charge of WHSmith's retail business. As someone who presides over a chain of 540 stores, with 17,000 staff, with annual sales of more than one billion pounds, she has a very big job and a very big salary package of around £500,000 to match. Also, in late 2000, there were even suggestions she would be in line to take over as chief executive of Smith's.

Beverley is bright. She got a 'first' from Cambridge in English. She is also used to breaking barriers and being number one. While at university she captained the tennis team. She is not someone who has been parachuted in at the top of WHSmith's from another career. She worked her way through many aspects of the business in an 18-year career at Boots and ended up as the first female managing director of a business in Boots' history when she became head of the Children's World stores.

Beverley's status is apparent because it was she who was chosen to head Smith's fightback out of a period in the doldrums in the 1990s when it had been overtaken by Waterstone's in bookselling.

♀

She came less than five years ago from Boots to bring 'energy' and with a brief of turning around Smith's with its 'stodgy, bureaucratic image' into a 'vibrant, less hierarchical and more entrepreneurial business'.

This is where her skills picked up from earlier retail experience come into play. Beverley was wrapped up in the selling culture from an early age when she first worked for the family printing and stationery business. Then as a sales and marketing controller for the National Theatre of Great Britain she got the taste for dealing with the public.

Beverley has fond memories of this job. She remembers how holiday jobs at the National Film Theatre and a gap year from her studies at Cambridge working for the National Theatre opened the door. 'It was a very exciting time. The company was expanding and we had three auditoria to fill instead of just one. It was my first job in middle-management and it gave me my first taste of marketing', she says.

In 1978 Beverley began at Boots as an assistant buyer in Bath. During the 1980s, she was promoted via a series of positions managing product areas. First, running the merchandising consultants in toiletries, then cosmetics. Then in 1984 she headed the introduction of in-store photo-processing labs to Boots, a business which now is worth £200 million a year in sales. From 1986 to 1989 she took another step up the ladder as merchandising and marketing controller for Beauty and pushed big-name perfume brands and expensive cosmetics like Estée Lauder on to the shelves for the first time in Boots.

For five years in the early 1990s Beverley headed home-care and music products, a division turning over £500 million a year.

Then in 1995 to 1996 she was deployed as a trouble-shooter as MD of Children's World and headed the decision by Boots to get rid of this business.

This is a period that taught Beverely a huge amount. First, it was a kind of 'wake-up call' into the cold and cruel realities of the business world for those who work near the top in big public companies. When Beverley took on the MD's role she did so not knowing that the Boots' top team had already talked about its sale. 'It became very clear, within weeks of me being there, that Children's World was going to need substantial financial investment. An invest-ment that Boots did not want to make.' Beverley says she has always much preferred working in areas where she can throw her energies in for the long term. When the new reality of her position was clear she reacted by re-focusing her energies. 'On the one hand, as a director I had to commit to getting the utmost value from the sale for share-holders. I also had an innate inclination of commitment to staff. I wanted to try and ensure alternative employment within the Boots group or with the future Children's World owner.'

'Second, the sale of that business taught me just how tough it can be in business. Initially, I had to keep secret the plans, even from my own financial director. I really hated not being able to be open and upfront with my staff and not being able to talk', Beverley recalls.

The Children's World chain, with 2,700 staff, was sold to Mothercare for about £60 million. 'I get enormous satisfaction from being a "clearer up of messes". Looking back, this episode in my career did teach me that I could be a so-called change agent', Beverley reflects.

After cutting her teeth in the role of a 'hit-woman' it was time for Beverley to move on to a new challenge.

For the next two years, Beverley became a director of British Shoe Corporation and was MD of its Dolcis and Cable & Co fashion chains at a time when they needed 'a radical repositioning'.

Then as sales and marketing controller for the National Theatre of Great Britain she got the taste for dealing with the public.

♀

From all these experiences, Beverley won the reputation of being someone who is very, very, in tune with customers. Staff observe her as someone who is always seeing things from the customer's perspective. 'I am passionate about retailing. In terms of my track record, I am seen as a "change agent" capable of re-inventing businesses and shaking them up', she says.

Part of Beverley's role as head of WHSmith Retail is to head Smith's fightback in the book market. She was still at Boots when Smith's first bought out the Waterstone's chain and then sold it to HMV Media but she can see how the decision to sell Waterstone's was a kind of turning point for Smith's. 'It enabled us to rebuild in popular books rather than academic and reference type books. My view is we are not there as a publishers' outlet, or even there for the authors, but for the customers. Retailing has to be more sensory-rich. If not, customers will say "why don't we just stay at home?". I am passionate in trying to be accessible about books, reading and writing. This means using Smith's weight to put colourful, exciting new things in front of the consumer. Doing for us in books what the top grocers did for the wine trade.'

Specifically, this means Smith's has brightened up its stores and introduced new gimmicks, like reading areas.

It also means Smith's made books 'very much its leading area' so that they account for between 25 to 30 per cent of the group's turnover while the other main areas of newspapers, music and stationery are 'relatively static'. During the year ended August 2000, WHSmith said its books business saw a 7 per cent sales increase in a generally flat market. In late 2000, Beverley Hodson was also deeply involved in a move to try and bring back 'top shelf' magazines to WHSmith news shelves. But this idea, motivated by commercial grounds, was pulled.

Her group is also fighting the online game with WHSmith Online and this carries a choice of 1.4 million books and is number two behind Amazon.com in online book sales. Furthermore, Smith's bought publisher Hodder Headline for £192 million, which had a strength in popular fiction and was its number four biggest supplier, and installed Tim Hely Hutchinson on its main board. Commercially, Smith's is making a comeback. Hodson says it has around 20 per cent of all books physically bought in shops in the UK. At a lowpoint in its fortunes in the mid-1990s, Smith's overall market share was down to 14 to 15 per cent.

One of her new ideas has been to introduce a 'Read of the Week' in stores. 'I don't select them, but I am part of setting the strategy, looking ahead like a kind of captain of the business.'

'In areas where we have used our market leader position to back certain authors and influence the trade, for instance with Delia Smith and Jamie Oliver in cookery, our share has climbed to 40 per cent', she said.

♀

Beverley, 48, is married and has children. She recognises the demands on her time are heavy, but, by talking to her, you pick up that she has a kind of secret weapon under her belt and that is a passionate belief in her area of retailing. This helps her 'swallow' very long hours.

'Retailing is a 24-hour, seven-day-a-week business. You have to be there when the customers want you to be there, and that is all the time!'

There is something of the workaholic about Beverley. 'I do get carried away with work and feel I just want to do more of it. I see that you have to be tough, passionate and have commitment', she says. When you meet her, you get the impression that she is a person who doesn't suffer fools gladly, though she stresses she also cares about her staff having fun in their work. 'As a boss I'm a bit variable. I'm not the worst person in the world, yet I'm demanding in certain ways, things like accuracy and thoroughness. But I'm also fairly informal. I can get out of my box if I don't think something is being done properly.'

Beverley also relates how she makes friends with and stays loyal to staff who do a good job for her. Like how she had an excellent PA in her days at Boots who lacked confidence to be promoted. 'Over time, I succeeded in persuading her to move up as a manager. Recently, she wrote back and told her about how she had got her first company car. 'I was very happy about that – if a person is ready to move up you should push them to something else. Otherwise you're being selfish', Beverley says.

For her, one of the thrills of her trade and a drive behind being in management is 'to motivate, enthuse and direct more staff to get a demonstrable buzz out of being creative. We have to work very hard to think up new reasons for customers to keep coming to us.'

Beverley has straightforward views on why women have made breakthroughs in her profession. 'It is simply because retailing is about people. This is more interesting to me and to most women than engineering gadgets.'

'I have a very strong value set. I wouldn't do it if there was slave labour involved, or exploiting children. I like selling products that make life better, not just about flogging things like shirts to make money. The idealistic bit of me is turned on and likes being in this branch of retailing rather than selling buckets of creosote.' Selling books is, she thinks, 'Selling magic in covers. It is like feeding people's minds and dreams in the same way that grocers feed people's stomachs.'

♀

So, women and the shopping business have a track record together.

It is also possible that retailing itself benefits from attitudes and skills that women can bring. At the most basic level, this has to be true since more than half of the country's customers are women.

In Britain over the last decade or so there has been explosive growth in the 'Do-it-Yourself' and home improvement side of the retail industry. The Homebase chain, developed by Sainsbury, and during the year 2000 sold by the stores group, benefited from this growth as it claimed a 12 per cent market share in the UK. Sainsbury's decided to sell Homebase because it wanted to raise around £1 billion in cash and concentrate on its core supermarkets business. After months of negotiations, its wish was all but granted just before Christmas 2000 when, in a deal worth more than £700 million, 72 per cent of the business was sold to Schroder Ventures and Kingfisher, while Sainsbury's kept a minority 18 per cent stake.

Kate Swann, Homebase's young, female boss until 2001, might ultimately be a beneficiary in terms of her career. She moved on to become managing director of the bigger Argos mail-order and cut-price goods retailer and claim another high-profile role in British retailing.

The Argos group provides a more expansive challenge for Kate Swann. It includes 450 stores and the combined turnover tops £2 billion compared with the £1.4 billion at Homebase. 'It is bigger and broader and in more sectors and that is very exciting for me. For instance, Argos sells toys and that is a completely new area for me.' One of her first tasks in 2001 has been heading the launch of a new fashion catalogue which added 30,000 new fashion lines for men, women and children. 'Argos will now cover virtually everything. With the exception of looking for food, shoppers won't really need to shop anywhere else', Kate told me.

Kate Swann is one of the country's most up-and-coming female entrepreneurs. In her early 30s, she became managing director of the 300 or so stores in the Homebase chain and was in charge of rolling out new megastores. Although the DIY craze has been bubbling away quietly since the 1960s, it is now one of the liveliest sectors of the economy. Incredible popularity of TV shows, on all channels, but led by shows like BBC's *Changing Rooms*, has fuelled an explosion in the market. Add in the gardening boom, and annual sales are worth around £30 billion.

Kate Swann says consumers are demanding more and more choice and ever-increasing product ranges. People are travelling abroad more and people's horizons have widened. So where the typical DIY store throughout the UK used to have 25,000 products on offer, they now have 45,000, she says. In the new 10,000 sq m (100,000 sq ft) megastores she helped to roll out, this product range rises to above 50,000 different items. 'We wanted to be more than a DIY store, we wanted to be a lifestyle store which reflected how home improvement has become a primary leisure activity', she said about how she viewed Homebase's role.

As the youngest person to ever head a business division at Sainsbury's, she felt her appointment was indicative of the way the stores giant tried to change its philosophy and bring in a fresh generation with new ideas.

'DIY was a lot less glamorous ten years ago', she admits.

Indeed, Swann started out as a graduate trainee for Tesco on the health and beauty product side. She moved to CocaCola and rose to become general manager in charge of marketing for all fizzy drinks in the UK. Swann was then headhunted by the Dixons Group and made their national marketing director for its Currys electrical chain.

At Homebase, she did detect a change in culture. 'In the past, DIY used to be male dominated and this was reflected in the senior management. Now it is a pursuit that has become one that is done on purely functional grounds. It is a sector of shopping, driven by the TV coverage, that is now more inspirational and aspirational and women do have more say.' The business is much more about women as well and she presided over a 30 strong senior management team at Homebase, at least half of which are women.

Kate Swann believes the role of mothers and women in the home lends itself to skills that are invaluable in store management. 'Women in their homes are used to managing lots of demands and juggling trade-offs between things. Consumers are becoming more demanding in terms of delivery methods, with options via the net, mail-order and direct from stores. Being in business requires keeping loads of different balls in the air', Swann says.

At Argos, she has arrived in a group that: 'Has a culture that is very open to change since the business was taken over by Great Universal Stores in 1998. There are a higher proportion of women at senior levels.'

As managing director, she often has to visit stores at weekends. 'Otherwise I would not get a flavour of trading on the busiest day of the week.'

How does she personally cope? 'For me, I don't mind getting up early. If you lead any sizeable business you have to be prepared to give up a lot of your life. At Argos now, I have a "very substantial" salary. I don't expect to get anything for nothing.' Kate says if she had one wish that could be granted it would be to cope with getting just five hours sleep a night, rather than the six or so she gets and feels is not quite enough to prevent her feeling 'grumpy'.

'Traditional bricks and mortar businesses now have to move very fast and developing the net-shopping side of the business at Homebase was like being a start-up entrepreneur for me.'

So would she see herself at the very top? 'In my career over the last couple of years, I would have to say to myself: "I've got enough on my plate". But, yes, I would like an absolute top role', Swann confided, when asked about her ambitions. Her move to be managing director of Argos, with its greater retailing scope, might prove to be another stepping stone in the direction of the top.

Beverley Hodson, as we know, and others, are attracted to retail because of the people element of the industry.

It also appears that retail may be attracted to women managers. And for those with ambition, it is possible that retailing will provide a route for women to the very top.

# 5

# *Media Queens*

The glitzy media world has allowed women to shine. From publishing, to television and the press and to public relations, women have not just felt life at the top, they have even commanded the top. Here, as we shall see from some of the most famous media women, is a world where the female sex has advantages. Women do bring skills that the media world appreciates. This means women have been recruited in great numbers for decades. Entrepreneurial and ambitious women have been attracted to make their own livings out of covering the lives of the glitterati and the famous. And in increasing numbers women are now top of the tree.

The world of glossy magazines and women editors go hand-in-hand. The fit is natural given that women are the main customers of magazines that, to a large degree, cater for perceived 'women's interests'. Sally O'Sullivan, who was editor-in-chief at the magazine giant IPC, who launched titles like *Good Housekeeping* and who launched her own publishing company Cabal Communications, is one of the most well known in the UK. Anna Wintour, as editor of *Vogue* in New York, has an international name.

Eve Pollard made headlines of her own when she became part of the most famous media marriage of editors of national newspapers. Her story is fascinating. She became editor of the *Sunday Express* when married to the long-serving editor of the *Daily Express*, another media heavyweight, Sir Nicholas Lloyd. As editor of the *Sunday Express* in the 1990s she paved the way for Rosie Boycott and Janet Street-Porter to also grab the editor's chair at 'nationals'. Also Rebekah Wade, at just 31, was able to become the youngest ever national editor when she grabbed the top spot at the *News of the World* and she followed the likes of Patsy Chapman, Bridget Rowe and Wendy Henry to edit Sunday tabloids.

Rosie Boycott, like Pollard, was adept at attracting headlines for herself when she backed the pro-cannabis lobby when in charge of *The Independent* and earned the nickname 'Rizla Rosie'. Boycott moved from the Indy to the editor's chair at the *Daily Express*, where she again was faced with the thankless task of running a paper with gloomy prospects. In the case of the *Express*, the paper carried a 'For Sale' tag for months on end.

Boycott said about this unsettling period at Britain's fourth biggest selling paper: 'We are in complete hiatus. We are probably halfway through a five-year plan. We need time and money and a good deal of commitment to bring it to fruition.'

The turmoil continued when the Express titles were eventually bought by down-market publisher, Richard Desmond, and when Rosie Boycott was replaced as editor.

♀

Eve, nicknamed 'La Bollard' on The Street, had ample personality of her own to suggest she would have made it anyway. Tales from those who worked under her suggest she was well-versed in using her big feminine credentials and also in cultivating an image to match her personality to help her on her way to the top. According to a head of commercial advertising at Express Newspapers who worked under her: 'Eve would charm the birds from the trees to get her own way'.

But, as editor, she had a reputation as a poor manager of staff and went through 25 personal assistants during her career. Also, Eve, whose well-endowed frame took a coutured size-18 dress, would recognise the importance of presenting the right image for potential commercial backers, and order specially-designed dresses with a size-12 label showing.

There are tales of her two very different personalities. On the one hand 'utterly charming' and on the other having a leadership style akin to a Sherman tank in being 'browbeating, bullying, intimidating and utterly humiliating'.

Eve Pollard made it to the top of the media world by being an editor. However, when she later set up in business with her own company, Parkhill Publishing, it folded after only a few months. Eve's publishing venture launched the glossy *Aura* magazine aimed at a supposed gap in the market for 40-something women still interested in sex, high-maintenance lifestyles and fashions. Those who worked on *Aura* and its sister title *Wedding Day* pointed to Eve's personal attitudes and management failings as a reason for the sudden demise in autumn 2000.

One top journalist, Chrissy Ilcy, called the Nick Lloyd and Eve Pollard partnership 'an amusing but sinister double act' and said they had 'a cavalier and arrogant' outlook. 'Her ego went into overdrive. Board meetings were a shambles. She refused to allow anyone to set up a management structure. No one ever doubted her energy, her terrific tabloid instincts, her gift for promotion and her ability to get people to do things for her. She slapped flattery on with a trowel if she needed you. But did she have management skills?' said former contributing editor Marcelle D'Argy Smith. This failure by Eve Pollard shows that there are different attributes needed to be a commercial success at the very head of a business.

♀

National newspapers are usually well-established publications. However, new editors, especially women, are often brought in when the title is looking tired, sales are falling and the paper is in need of a re-branding. Editors have undoubted influence on current events, politics and the mood of the country. They have staffs of hundreds and customers, in terms of readers, of millions.

But the editors cannot compare with the entrepreneurial publishers and press barons in terms of commercial impact. And so for real power in business, we need to explore the lives of our 'publishing queens'.

♀

Gail Rebuck, as UK chief executive of the Random House Group publishing empire, has been called the 'First Lady of UK publishing'. Her book businesses read like a roll-call of the famous publishing imprints from Jonathan Cape, to Century and Chatto and Windus and turnover at Random House tops £200 million. And the 'first lady' tag is not without irony as Gail is married to Philip Gould, the media consultant at the heart of Tony Blair's Labour government.

Gail, after first graduating from Sussex University and time working in a clothes shop, says about her first steps in the publishing world: 'I started off as a humble production assistant in a children's book packager called Grisewood & Dempsey. I then moved to Robert Nicholson Publications, launched a paperback list for the Hamlyn Group and was one of the founder directors of Century along with Anthony Cheetham, he mortgaged his flat and I did as well.'

Century, a small publisher when it was started in 1982, was a significant launchpad for Gail's career. 'I was not a humble editor but the Publisher of the non-fiction list', she says.

Among her authors was the famed management guru Charles Handy, a figure who she says became a kind of mentor to her, along with co-founder Anthony Cheetham.

During the early 1980s Century grew and eventually struck a merger deal with Hutchinson in 1985. Following Hutchinson, I also took on the Rider list and the Business list, followed by the Ebury list when we acquired it, says Gail.

Then in 1989 Random House swallowed up Century Hutchinson and Gail, by then a director, made £1 million personally. By 1991 Gail Rebuck's ambitions meant she had manoeuvred from being the non-fiction publisher to chief executive of the new publishing giant. When her former mentor Anthony Cheetham resigned as chief executive, Rebuck is said to have known his fate a week before he did. She says about replacing him: 'It felt terrible. There are things I have had to do that I feel deeply uncomfortable about.' And on the job itself, she said it was 'like moving to Mars'. The job involved a very steep learning curve and it probably would not have gone to her as a woman had Random House not been a US-owned publisher with a different culture, she believes. Gail has remained chief executive following a takeover of Random by the German media colossus Bertlesmann in 1997 and her job sees her in charge of 1,800 staff in the UK, Australia, and South Africa. Following the subsequent takeover of Random House by Bertlesmann in 1997, she also took over the responsibility for Transworld, which includes imprints Bantam, Doubleday, Black Swan and Corgi.

When Gail first hit the top, she was stung by criticism that she had promoted women colleagues because they were women and not simply because she felt they were the best. This implies, even in the early 1990s, women making

waves near the top were still rare enough to warrant attention. And Gail remembers an occasion when top executives
gathered in the days after the joining with Bertlesmann
when 'I was one of only two women in a room full of 100
men'.

On her own attitude she claims: 'I tend to be very
straight in dealings. I ignore the fact that I am a woman.
Women don't have the sole proprietorship of intuitive and
listening skills and publishing is also about a passion and
instinct for books.' But one of the reasons why women
have moved on from the early days when they were merely
the secretaries in publishing is because it is a business that
requires 'keeping lots of balls in the air at the same time',
a skill that women are traditionally good at. 'Publishing is
a series of compromises. The crucial challenge is balancing
creativity and profitability', says Rebuck. Women emerging
more in the workplace is a facilitator that encourages innovation, and, according to Rebuck, competitiveness is about
innovation.

How does she personally cope with being a boss and a
mother? 'It is difficult, but not impossible. I find labels like
"Superwoman" incredibly unhelpful', she says. 'My job
entails a lot of reading and it can't all be done in the office.'

Gail will tell you that her secret for success lies in her
'passion for books'. 'I wouldn't be in publishing if I didn't
love books.' This means she reads a phenomenal amount.
When on holiday and not distracted by running the business she reads at least a book a day. 'My children always
used to draw pictures of me with a book in my face.'

In all her time as boss, Gail says she tries to encourage
flexibility. 'I don't give brownie points to people who stay
at the office very late at night.'

'I would never say that if people consistently stay late in
the office they should be fired. However, I do believe that
if people consistently stay late it is either because they are
not able to do their job or they are overworked. In which
case I need to do something about it.'

For her, the pressure of life at the top has 'crushed out some of the excitement of work'. As her career progressed, 'there is nothing in my life more thrilling than when a book worked', said Gail. However, she still gets a buzz out of her authors, claiming it to be a 'privilege' to be one of the first people to read a manuscript by a world famous author.

Gail says about becoming a woman chief executive and gaining the extra burdens that she will consider it worth it if: 'Only in some small way it changes the climate for women . . . and men'.

About the present climate, Gail says: 'It is not the liveliest period for book sales I've ever experienced, although I'm pleased Random sales have held up and outperformed the market.'

She says publishing has always been a small world. 'It is like living in a pressure cooker. You keep knocking into other publishers. We are going through a revolution in publishing. A revolution, that due to technology, is taking place with its finger on the fast-forward button', says Gail. 'The J. R. Hartley advert image is a thing of the past', she says, referring to the image of a long-forgotten author trying to track a copy of his long-forgotten work on fly-fishing through the *Yellow Pages*. 'Nowadays technology has meant the whole concept of an out-of-print book is over – you can publish on demand. Technology has also spawned e-readers which mean several manuscripts can be read in a much more portable way. Publishing in the UK is suffering a backlash from a period of over-expansion in bookshops. This first happened in the USA four or five years ago. This was led by Borders fighting Barnes & Noble to be on every High Street. There was overstocking and publishers were hit by huge returns of unwanted books from stores. We have to get together to ensure that books remain a sexy industry. For the young, we have to make reading exciting and make sure the activity is not forced into a dusty, fusty, library image.'

Rebuck, whose company publishes 2,000 titles a year, takes an ironic pleasure in watching people like Peter Kindersley, founder of CD-ROM publisher Dorling Kindersley and doom-monger on traditional books, fall by the wayside when it was taken over by Pearson. 'I have the greatest respect for Peter Kindersley, but, the book is here to stay', Rebuck says.

Apart from her publishing fame, Gail also is a very big campaigner to improve literacy in Britain. In 1998 she helped launch 'World Book Day', a campaign that saw 11 million children between the ages of five and 18 given a £1 book voucher. Her Random House business has sponsored its local comprehensive school near the HQ in Pimlico. Gail backed the charity Business In the Community in its 'Time to Read' campaign because, she says: 'Business has a real interest in a literate, well-educated, workforce'.

At about the same time, in summer 2000, that Blair's government scored several own goals with leaks from its advisory team, including from Gail's husband Gould, Rebuck's status as the first lady of publishing gained a challenger in the form of Victoria Barnsley as the new chief executive of HarperCollins. Gail claims that having a husband with a high profile in the political world has been 'neutral' on her own career. 'We work very independently. I don't let it interfere. That's the way madness lies but that's it as far as my attitude is concerned', she said. But we wonder how disingenuous Gail is being and we are left to wonder how many doors to political memoirs are opened.

What cannot be doubted is that the new boss of one of the very biggest UK publishers is an entrepreneurial 'boss woman' to rival Rebuck. The two obviously know each other well. In an amusing twist, Gail Rebuck and Victoria Barnsley have even used the same nanny to help make their own lives easier as they separately pursued their top publishing careers.

As Gail explains: 'Three years ago I had an application from a nanny through an agency I use regularly and I took her on. It turned out that her previous employer was Victoria. The nanny stayed with me for two years, leaving over a year ago. I didn't steal her, she applied for a job.'

'Victoria and I have been colleagues for years as Random House distributed Fourth Estate books. The distinguishing factor of all relationships in publishing tends to be collegiate and respectful and not adversarial', Rebuck says.

Victoria Barnsley began in Junction Books, a small publisher run by her old tutor that went bust in 1984. By borrowing money from friends and with the help of an £80,000 Business Expansion Scheme loan she set up her own fledgling publisher, Fourth Estate. Victoria's business was named small publishing house of the year 1990. A nomination for the Veuve Clicquot Businesswoman of the Year followed. Unlike Rebuck, there seems less of a passion for books about Victoria's make-up and more a fascination with making money. Said to be stimulated more by ambition than ideas, the editing side of publishing afforded her only mild satisfaction. 'The business side always interested me more, that was the real fun. I like playing with figures. I could have worked in a quite different field. I would have found it extremely interesting', she said.

Writers say about her that she is not a great originating publisher but brilliant or lucky at spotting long-shot winners and buying overseas rights. By the time of the merger with Harper, her Fourth Estate had turnover of £7.5 million, but the much larger Harper was turning over £124 million in the UK. The fact that Victoria Barnsley was immediately installed as the chief executive of the new merged business suggested to outsiders that the thinking behind the deal was really to land her as a boss. It also came after the Murdoch-owned HarperCollins had been going through several years of decline and when morale of its staff was low. Barnsley, who 'always wanted to work on a bigger canvas', found a timely home for her ambitions.

Meanwhile, there are publishing queens to be found elsewhere at the top of the book world. Alexandra Pringle is editor-in-chief at Bloomsbury, the publisher that is making millions on the back of its Harry Potter children's books by J. K. Rowling.

So why are women beginning to rule British publishing in the twenty-first century? Perhaps because publishing, more than other professions like engineering, has always needed females. 'Most of these top women started as entry-level gofers stuffing jiffy bags with books and asking men in Savile Row suits if they took milk and sugar in their drinks', says author John Sutherland. Also publishing has always been a career open to talent. Creative publishing is a mixture between nurturing and nagging. Many authors are like babies and women handle them well. Furthermore, the old gentlemanly world of publishing over long and expensive lunches and tapping 'the old boy network' is dying out and this opens the window to the women.

♀

Sally O'Sullivan has been called 'the doyenne of glossies'. And as chief executive of her own publishing start-up, Cabal Communications, is very much a figurehead. A boss far more well known for what she is, than what the business is.

No shrinking violet, she is adept at playing the media star role. Former *Sun* editor Kelvin MacKenzie described her as 'the finest magazine editor of her generation'. Not a bad compliment from a man who is hated for his quick to criticise attitude and his reputation for never bestowing compliments lightly, especially on women.

O'Sullivan also formed part of one of Britain's most famous media partnerships when she was, for several years, married to Charlie Wilson who edited seven papers in his career, including *The Times*, *The Independent* and the *Glasgow Herald*.

In the magazine world, she had already built up a star reputation through heading a string of glossies like *Harpers & Queen*, *Options*, *Ideal Home* and *She*. And at *Good Housekeeping* she took sales to half a million a month. Then, in the very early days of Cabal, she allowed in the BBC TV cameras to film a four-part series called *Trouble Between the Covers* that exposed her business, warts and all.

It also exposed the inflated egos of her staff and life-styles dominated by partying and sex. The programmes also showed the high staff turnover rates at Cabal and the pit-falls of being small and entrepreneurial and trying to fight on the same patch as the big established players. When Sally launched Cabal, she talked big and expressed a goal of unleashing a dozen new titles within the first year. She wanted to create a stir. The cameras caught the regular comings and goings of senior staff. Also how the dream fell well short of reality and only two new titles, *Real Homes* and *Front*, survived the early months. Another, *Good Health*, was quickly sold and other titles, like *Crime Weekly*, which saw its launch pulled, were dropped or put on indefinite 'hold'. Eighteen months after its birth, Cabal had added just two more of its own titles to the news stands, *Pro Cycling* and the men's lifestyle mag, *Mondo*.

Sally claimed the publicity 'did more good than harm'. This is either affirmation that all publicity is good publicity, or seeing things, with the benefit of Sally's years of media experience, with a slightly rose-tinted perspective. Nevertheless, she does have an eye for business oppor-tunities: 'Cabal is a small, young company in a highly competitive market place. We have two main revenue streams; copy sales and advertising. Two free hours of prime-time television gives us the type of exposure to the generators of those revenue streams that we simply couldn't afford to buy', she said.

Immediately prior to forming Cabal Communications, named after those people who form together in a secret plot, Sally was the most publicly-known person behind a management-led attempt at a £1 billion bid for IPC from publishing giant Reed Elsevier.

She said she had never conceived the possibility of doing the round with City banks to raise that kind of money. In a way, her experience reflected a 'typical female conundrum' in that women 'have all the brain, the drive and business acumen to spot the deal, but have some link missing that says "this deal will be mine", which is more natural in men'.

Sally started by leading the £1 billion attempted deal at IPC, but resigned because she was not prepared to see editorial directors given a lesser say and lesser ownership of share options than the directors from operational backgrounds. O'Sullivan lost that battle, but was not too disappointed and admits to feeling 'completely amazed that I had got so far'. Reed eventually sold its IPC consumer magazine business to a venture capital firm, Cinven.

It was at this stage the penny dropped for Sally. She wanted to control her own company. In comparison to the IPC bid, money needed for Cabal was 'minuscule' but Sally found it much harder to raise and eventually she tapped five rich friends for the handful of millions. 'The transition from the IPC bid to Cabal was, at worst a learning experience and at best the most exciting thing ever – forget Chanel and Sex! It taught me that a business is simply a jigsaw of talents. You have one and you fit the others around you', said Sally.

On a day-to-day basis, Sally would describe herself as a kind of 'mother hen' figure. 'I am trying to be overall guider and trying to let individual editors run their own shows', she said when Cabal kicked off in 1999.

About her management philosophy she says: 'In almost every company I've worked in, too many layers of management have stifled talent. Our idea is simple – identify the person you believe to be right for the job and assume they will do it brilliantly. Nineteen times out of twenty they will. On the twentieth, act quickly in whatever way is appropriate.'

Sally's new magazine company is young in itself and young in terms of staff with most under 30. Also Sally took pleasure in introducing radical, or wacky, new ideas on how to make her company the best. This included granting staff four 'mental health days' a year when they can ring up if they can't face work problems and simply take the day off to indulge themselves. Also founding staff were given their own budgets to go out and buy their own taste in office furniture. In the early days, everyone was given a bar of chocolate every Wednesday on the basis it was only half way through the week and something was needed to cheer you along.

Sally has interesting tips for those who want to be 'go-getters'. 'Work out exactly why you are starting your own business – it's always useful to keep in the back of your mind in the darker moments. Also don't be put off when people tell you how difficult it will be, or how brave you are being.' Sally believes knowing where to go to find answers is more important than trying to know everything yourself. 'You should pull every string you can. Trust your instincts. Take holidays – what's the point of being a good manager if you can't manage yourself?'

O'Sullivan, 51, has also experienced what it is like to be part of the so-called great and good. She sat on the Broadcasting Standards Commission, the Advisory Council on Drug Misuse and as a non-exec at Anglian Water. Though terrified at first and convinced she was 'finally going to get rumbled' she was surprised she 'had something to contribute'.

She claims that women are less driven about corporate life and don't care about companies as a goal in their lives in the same way as men do. 'I am as surprised as anyone that I am running my own company.'

But she does believe that women have things to offer saying: 'Women are good at networking in a more natural type of way. There should be a lot more women at the top in media.'

♀

The worlds of television and public relations have fed off each other so successfully in the last two decades that the whole profession of PR has grown into a significant industry.

First, TV tapped the image of PR as a fluffy, fun-filled, banal, profession that was outside the world of the vast majority of the population. By doing so TV, with *Absolutely Fabulous*, the PR comedy show that aped the life of one of the first household names in PR, Lynne Franks, was able to win huge audiences around the world. Who can say how many impressionable young things were encouraged into the growing profession as a result? In fact, public relations is the third most popular choice of industry among new graduates; and competition for places is tough.

No matter. The commercial world has now realised that public image does impact on the bottom line.

The public relations industry has been growing at between 14 per cent and 20 per cent a year over the last half dozen years. This growth is fuelled by a whole new communications industry that has grown up on the back of the Internet boom. According to the Public Relations Consultants Association, it is now an industry worth at least £1 billion annually.

This means more than 30,000 now work in public relations in the UK, with women far outnumbering men. The PRCA has 5,500 members who work in agency consultancies. It has seen fee income more than double from £146 million in 1990 to £350 million in 1999. The PRCA's figures also show that women in PR as a whole outnumber men by 70 per cent to 30 per cent. This predominance is not yet fully reflected in success at the top level, but in PR boardrooms women are beginning to be just as common as men.

'The explosion of the Public Relations consultancy business on both sides of the Atlantic has fostered the employment of women and their development as managers and directors. It has been a two-way process because women have increasingly targeted the communications sector in higher education as gender friendly and they have been welcomed by employers with opportunities for personal development and advancement that are lacking in traditional professions, manufacturing and engineering', says Tom Watson, Chairman, Public Relations Consultants Association. 'Women are at least equal to men in creativity, client handling, financial management and service delivery. It is rare to find a PR practitioner of any age who makes any differentiation on the grounds of gender, other than to comment that women outnumber men in the PR business', he said

As a result, the PR sector has been in the van of family-friendly policies that encourage women to return to employment after the birth of children. This, in turn, has led to the retention of many more women in their 30s and 40s who in other professions would have been lost forever. Policies such as part-time employment, job-share and maternity breaks are not controversial or difficult issues in public relations. They are norms of employment practice.

Because PR has been an area of business where women have been welcomed as equals and because the industry is actively improving management training, the future looks bright. According to Tom Watson: 'The next area for women to reach parity with male colleagues is at senior management level, especially with the international networks. At present, there are relatively few women CEOs in major international PR groups, although at national level

63

there are many women entrepreneurs who have developed very successful, expanding businesses. This will change in time and women will become as well known in senior positions as their male colleagues.

Possibly the main drive will come with changes in management education in the PR business. Up to the end of the twentieth century, the training emphasis was on public relations skills – craft, planning, strategy and client service. Now the sustained growth of the business is calling for management training to continue expansion in international markets. In the UK, the PRCA is introducing a Diploma in Consultancy Management that offers opportunities for women to expand their horizons. This is expected to become an essential tool for aspiring consultancy managers and is likely to be imitated around the world. Women will take a very full part in management training and this will enable their step into the highest levels of responsibility, alongside male colleagues who have been trained in management and accountancy earlier in their careers', the PR industry chief explained.

'The future for women of all ages in public relations is excellent and sustainable through undergraduate, in-house and post-graduate training as well as family-friendly policies. PR's own public relations has genuine strengths that are good for its own future', he said.

♀

In Lesley Smith and Sue Farr we can see how the PR profession has provided a route to the top.

Lesley Smith is Corporate Affairs Director at Dixons, where she is ultimately in charge of the image of one of our biggest stores groups with an annual turnover of £4 billion.

Sue Farr has joined the list of those women who are boss in the agency side of the PR profession. After a high profile career at the BBC, she has become managing director of Golin Harris International. From her London base, she is in charge of Europe, the Middle East and Africa for the top-twenty global agency.

Lesley Smith has had a fascinating career. In the 1980s early in her PR career, she was one of only a handful of women to tread the corridors of power at Westminster when she was a press officer for the Labour Party in the days·when women political editors and senior advisers to ministers in Parliament could be counted without running out of fingers. She later worked her way to the top with stints at the Burson-Marsteller agency and Railtrack before becoming a huge 'voice' in the commercial world as a board director for the Dixons, Currys and PC World chains and by being on the board of the British Retail Consortium.

Lesley, in her Labour Party days, was one of the driving forces behind women-only shortlists for candidates to be MPs and also a leading campaigner for the principle of 'One Member, One Vote' in party policy-making. 'When I worked at Westminster in the late 1980s and early 1990s, there were only four women Lobby journalists and I was one of only two women working in PR for political parties', recalls Lesley. 'The advantage of this is we were very, very, visible. You couldn't help but be noticed. Even now, some eight years after finishing working at Westminster full-time, the policemen, gate-keepers and gallery staff still recognise me. Without doubt, this has helped give my career a boost. Things have changed, there are more women now. But with the old Fleet Street press community a thing of the past, the Westminster Lobby and press gallery is the only place where a "village atmosphere" still exists', she says.

Lesley does recognise there are disadvantages to being a woman in the media world and in the corporate world. In circumstances where 'being noticed and being taken notice of are important it is a drawback . . . if you are, say, in your late 30s, and about five foot two. A lack of sheer physical presence means it is difficult to get noticed in the way a man who is six foot or so and bulky never has to worry about.'

Lesley's tip to aspiring communications go-getters who want to stand out in a crowd is: 'Take care and choose carefully who you first enter a packed reception with'.

There may be something in 'arm furniture', as favoured by the glitterati, after all!

♀

In the opinion of Lesley, the reason why women have made great strides towards the top in the PR world is because the demands of modern working life are much more stringent. 'The job of a Corporate Affairs Director has changed out of all recognition. In the old days, a seat at the Top Table could be filled by old buffers, who got there after dozens of years of service in the same company and who could have been the chairman's henchmen. Now, the job at a vast corporation has vast responsibilities, it is much bigger and requires many skills. Women do have these skills and they can come in at board level as experts in communication', she thinks.

Lesley is well-qualified to offer an opinion on how corporate life is in comparison with political life. 'Without doubt, life in commerce is much tougher. It is much more intellectually challenging.'

One of her greatest difficulties is handling the feeling of isolation that all women at the pinnacle of businesses feel. 'At Dixons, I have only one girly mate on a par anywhere near me, that's Elizabeth Fagan in charge of marketing at second-tier board level. Otherwise, it is a room filled by 16 men.' Lesley says men and women in team-building positions should be open enough to appoint people who are better than themselves. She has first hand experience of how difficult it is to overcome male prejudice. 'When I was at Railtrack, I got labelled as someone who only hired women. But in reality, when you look back, the new appointments were fifty-fifty between the sexes.'

'As a woman, you have to be twice as good to be seen as half as good', Lesley says on reflecting about her career to date. However, once you prove yourself, PR and communications offer great opportunities to a woman.

♀

Sue Farr made her name in a ten-year career in marketing and PR in the British television industry. In the early 1990s she was director of Corporate Communications for independent commercial television channel, Thames TV. She then broke new ground by becoming the first professional marketer for the public service BBC. When she headed publicity for BBC Radio in 1993, the prevailing culture at the organisation had been that such work was 'rather vulgar'. By 1999 she had been promoted to be the director in charge of the whole range of public service marketing for the BBC.

Claire Walker, by comparison, as managing director of Firefly Communications, an agency with £6 million in annual fees, is typical of those who rode to the top after building her own specialist, hi-tech, agency.

Claire, aged 37, was so keen to run her own business she shunned the normal route of gaining better qualifications and instead pulled out of plans for 'A' levels and left school at 16. She set up Firefly in 1990 and she still owns 70 per cent and in 1999 she made £1.2 million in salary and share sell-offs. Looking back on her incredible success story she says; 'My timing was perfect. PR was booming, technology was booming – so I entered a double bubble.'

In a parallel way, greater commercialisation and expansion of broadcasting has created many more opportunities for women to come out on top in the media.

Also, slowly but steadily, the BBC has being undergoing a revolution. Lorraine Heggessey, described as a 'ball of fire' in days as head of factual programmes at the broadcasting corporation, was promoted and made controller of BBC 1. Today, about a third of the BBC's senior management is female. But this success comes after long years of women being in the wilderness. In 1984 the BBC had launched a major inquiry into why so few women had top jobs and in 1990, John Birt, later to become director-general, introduced an anti-sexism database and the first high-profile breakthrough came when Jane Root was made controller of BBC 2 in 1998.

Dawn Airey was made controller of the new Channel 5 in her mid-30s, a role that means she is one of the most influential and powerful people in TV in terms of commissioning and scheduling of programmes. Interestingly, Dawn Airey went on the same type of Harvard Business school course that also helped Greg Dyke to the top at the BBC. She had always wanted to run her own channel and expressed an interest in becoming a business head on top of a creative head and in late 2000 she was made chief executive of Channel Five. She says her gender is irrelevant in the eyes of her staff, though there is 'a residual bitchiness in the TV industry as a whole that she might have risen too far too fast'.

Denise O'Donoghue is a beneficiary of the huge rise in power of the independent production companies in the TV world. Denise founded in 1986, and rose to become chairman of, Hat Trick Productions which made over £1 million a year at its peak when it was famed for making programmes like *Have I Got News for You?* and *Drop the Dead Donkey*. Denise says: 'When I started, independent production companies were on the margins of TV and I was able to succeed as the situation changed and we became much more important.' She also tells tales of 'being talked over' by men in the industry when she started out and says 'I wouldn't have achieved any of this had I not set Hat Trick up myself'.

The radio has also planted the seeds for female media bosses. Jenny Abramsky became head of News for the BBC after a 25-year career that began as a studio hand and saw her become editor of programmes known throughout the world like the *Today* programme, *The World at One* and *PM* on the serious news channel Radio Four. Abramsky, who also launched radio Five Live and who is director of Radio for the BBC, has used her position to act as a mentor for other women and she chose Helen Boaden, 44, to be the new controller of Radio Four. Abramsky, 53, says: 'The environment I work in is tough and unsociable and it is a real obligation to ensure it is a working culture in which women can flourish. We must have a workforce that reflects the population that we are broadcasting for. When I was first made an editor in the BBC I was the only woman, which I found profoundly depressing.'

Sue Farr succeeded Julia Thorn when she retired in 2001 from the top job at Golin Harris in the UK. Through their careers they both show how women's skills and attitudes have grown to be recognised.

Sue is: 'Great at building teams and she then makes you feel you are working with her rather than for her', according to a former BBC PR client. And Sue says she tries to be inclusive in her own management style. 'The control and command management style is dead, thank God', she says.

As Julia Thorn points out: 'In the PR world today there are no barriers to women and women undoubtedly have good skills to offer. But when I started, I very much wondered if, as a woman, clients would ever take me seriously. For a long time, women were stuck at the second tier level. Even 10 to 15 years ago in PR women felt they did all the work while the men took the glory.'

Julia then remembers how barriers began to break down after Margaret Thatcher became the first woman prime minister. 'Thatcher was inspiring to me, although I didn't like politics. It gave me a confidence by association. By watching her, I realised I could manage as well.'

♀

Julia Thorn began her path to success in the media world, as many others did, as a lowly cub reporter. Armed with three 'A' levels, she left school and went straight into work without a university degree, like so many of her generation who are now in their 50s. Her first job was on the *Slough Observer* and she then switched to the more seedy and, in career terms, much more challenging patch of the *South East London Mercury*. Here she remembers the high crime rate and how she also built up a reputation as an 'Action Girl' and used to report on a variety of media stunts.

'Journalism was a crash course in life' for her. However, Julia became fed up with what she calls the 'manufacturing of stories out of nothing and the entrapment'. Journalists to this day will also empathise with her feeling fed up with a life of 'hard work and no pay'.

This desire to find a better way of making a living took Julia into the world of corporate communications for Marks and Spencer and then, in 1981, she first joined her agency, Paragon. It is here that Julia's rise went in tandem with the new growth industry of the 1980s, corporate publishing, and the Paragon business itself grew to one employing more than 100 at its peak and it gained its own stock market listing before being swallowed up into the Shandwick empire.

Julia Thorn, unlike a lot of chief executives, had a style which was very 'hands on'. Staff will tell you how she was a visible figure around their desks even though Thorn's 'boss' role meant new dimensions of international office politics had accumulated onto her plate. Her experience of being in at the start of the boom in corporate publishing means that when she acts as 'mother' to provide critical guidance at rehearsals for new business pitches to try and win new staff magazine accounts, her views of what impression the prospective client will get are well-informed.

Indeed Julia's own motivation for becoming a boss stems not from a desire to climb higher but more from an innate belief she could do the job better. In her own words; 'more rebellion than ambition. I never liked having bosses.' And in her own experience, women in PR are very focused and because of this they do the job well and because of this, promotion follows.

The Golin Harris agency and corporate publishing business has fee income of around £4 million annually. With 25 or so clients with blue chip names like Lloyds TSB and BAA she claims her firm's influence, like others in communications, is disproportionately higher than any fee measurement. 'The industry is changing. Public Relations is now an item on the bottom line in its own right where before it was just swallowed up as part of a marketing budget.'

Julia Thorn worked on the team that put the Orange phone service brand on the map. She also relates how, when she goes to the airports, she can look around and see clients' names, from Heathrow to the suitcase maker Samson to the bank cash machines, and this 'gives me sheer pleasure out of being aware of the influence we have'.

Julia says she personally has not encountered sexism from within the PR agency world; 'though some clients have had a funny idea of what constitutes PR and what our services should include!' And Julia is not adverse to playing on men's weakness for the female sex. 'If it helps to flutter the eyelids to win clients, then go for it', she says. Quite! In the media world, sex does sell.

# 6

# On Top, Over Here

Marjorie Scardino, as chief executive of media giant Pearson plc, is the most powerful woman in business in Europe. Indeed, she is rated the most powerful and influential woman in Britain. She ranked well above The Queen in a recent top 300 'Power List' compiled by the *Observer* and Channel Four. Marjorie was rated the seventeenth most powerful person, while our Monarch came in at a more lowly seventy-fourth and Prime Minister's wife Cherie Blair was a more respectable forty-eighth.

Scardino is the only woman to hold the title of Chief Executive at one of our top 100 companies. As such, she presides over a group valued on the stock market at more than £12 billion and a group that owns some of the best-known names in the media, like *The Financial Times*, Penguin Books and Thames TV.

When Scardino was appointed to lead Pearson in 1997 the news raised many eyebrows in the financial world. Pearson had long been one of the most blue-blooded British institutions with interests at the time stretching beyond the FT to include Lazards investment bank and Madame Tussauds, however it had reached a low ebb 'financially, commercially and spiritually'. It was clear it needed new leadership, but what took people aback was the choice of an unknown American woman who was under 50 at the time and who was accused of lacking the clout or experience necessary.

When she took over at Pearson, Scardino said she would turn the place upside down if necessary and said: 'I'm unconventional. I'm pretty brave about things like that'.

♀

Scardino, has, in short, proved many doubters wrong. She has led an amazing shake-out of businesses and with the help of billions worth of acquisitions brought a new focus to Pearson and its share price doubled in three years after she took over. Marjorie herself has benefited and become one of the top twenty richest women in Britain with a £2.7 million package in 1999–2000, including a special £1.5 million bonus and share options.

What is interesting is how Scardino as an individual can be taken to symbolise how business women from the USA have a very much better track record in reaching the top than their counterparts from this country.

Scardino has a background of coming from relative obscurity to grab top positions. She is a Texan from the deep-south of America with a southern drawl to match. Her first break came when she was 23 and made news editor at news agency Associated Press's bureau in West Virginia. It was here she met her future husband Albert who was then just a reporter, but who later went on to win a Pullitzer prize. The two shared an anger at the political divides in the American South and between them tried reviving the *Georgia Gazette* in his home town of Savannah. This first venture into the business end of publishing was not a total success, they racked up $250,000 debts which were not repaid until 1995, but it did provide a launching pad. Scardino's husband got a job on the *New York Times* and she followed him to run *The Economist* in the USA.

Having doubled that magazine's circulation in the USA she was transferred to the London head office as chief executive of The Economist Group. Pearson had a stake in the Economist business, but this on its own did not explain how Scardino got promoted to the very top. One clue may be Scardino becoming a director of the Periodical Publishers Association as this provided one avenue for her networking and desire to meet influential people.

♀

Another reason why she leapfrogged over well-qualified candidates already on the Pearson board was that the group wanted a clean break from the past. Scardino, in the eyes of the establishment, was seen as having strength in her foreignness and having a gutsy and feisty image and was defined as an American first and then a woman. Timing was therefore on her side when the Pearson leadership came, but this alone does not explain why she was in the frame in the first place.

Scardino is said to be an outstanding presenter and as such is good at relations with the City. She is publicity-shy as far as outsiders are concerned, but does have a famed 'personal touch' towards the 20,000 or so staff in the group and this runs to writing in cuddly detail in the company magazine and asking staff their opinions. Above all, she has shown what it takes to make tough decisions. She has been likened to a market trader in the way she bought and sold businesses. Since 1997, this has seen the disastrous Mindscape consumer software business sold for $150 million and the more frivolous parts of the Pearson empire go, like the Port Aventura theme park in Spain and the world-famous Madame Tussauds tourist attractions business sold for £350 million. In June 1999 Pearson sold its shareholdings in the Lazards investment bank for £410 million.

Also there has been expansion of the FT and expansion of Pearson television interests in Europe and in her native America at the cost of hundreds of millions and the purchase of the educational and professional book publisher Simon & Schuster for £2.9 billion. Pearson also bought National Computer Systems for £1.7 billion, a business that sells educational aids to US schools. And outside life at Pearson, Marjorie Scardino was also appointed as a director to the US-owned Internet giant AOL.

Scardino has a maxim on the way she works and that is: 'Have a plan, execute it violently and do it today'.

♀

When Scardino was parachuted to the top of Pearson in 1997 she was following a trail set a couple of years before when the Laura Ashley fashion and fabrics group appointed another American woman, Ann Iverson, as its chief executive. Another American, Barbara Cassani, was also given the plum job of being the chief executive of British Airways' brand new low-cost fares 'Go' airline in 1997.

Ann Iverson had a well-established reputation in retail in her native USA and in Britain before being thrust into the Laura Ashley hot seat. Her rise and fall is a fascinating tale that we shall look at later. Also Barbara Cassani's rise from a starting point of an 'Ivy League' education in the USA is worth studying. But for now, what is of interest is how many other American women have risen to the top in business before them and why the culture in the USA has been so different to the UK's.

♀

The British attitude to those who are successful and rich may be changing. But, it has a long way to go when compared with the culture in the USA which hands out hero status to those who have got rich by their own efforts. Though speaking tongue-in-cheek, Mike Lynch, the boss of Autonomy, the UK's largest Internet software business, summed up this attitude by saying: 'There used to be a joke doing the rounds. If you started a business in Hong Kong, your family would run it. If you started it in California, your friends would buy equity. If you did it in the UK, people would tell you that you couldn't succeed and then scratch your car when you did.'

Peggy Dannenbaum has experienced at first hand what it is like to be an entrepreneur in the UK. Though American by birth, her whole business career has been in Britain and she lives in London with her family of four. Peggy's first claim to fame was, she says, introducing Ciabatta bread to a wider range of consumers through a deal with the Marks and Spencer chain. She later took a non-executive role at Thornton's plc and was vice-chair of the NHS Wellhouse Trust.

However, her biggest business challenge is happening now. Peggy is chair and chief executive of Veos plc, a fledgling company that is behind the introduction of a revolutionary new contraceptive for women. Veos joined the stock market in 1999 and raised £20 million to finance the project to introduce its 'Oves' cap-like contraceptive that is made out of silicon and is likened to a 'contact lens for the cervix'. In the couple of years before the product's nationwide launch in the year 2001, Peggy has seen her company's value double and then halve again to 75p in tune with the wild fluctuation in fortunes of the biotechnology sector of the stock market.

'In the USA, making money for yourself and being in business is a highly respected thing. Socially it is more prestigious to make your own money than to have inherited it. Until very recently Bill Gates was a hero!', says Peggy.

'In the USA there are huge numbers of entrepreneurial women. They often wind up getting training in the large corporations and then going and setting up on their own.' She thinks: 'It is quite difficult in the UK to raise venture capital money and even more difficult if you are a woman'.

Peggy's view is that most businesses in the USA are started with individual 'business angel' money. This money comes from entrepreneurs who have already made it themselves. Business angels who are keen to give others a chance, but also business angels who are prepared to risk investing in 20 start-ups with the reality that only one will really take off. 'The attitude is "give others a better chance by giving *my brains and my funds*"', she said.

According to the US Global Entrepreneurship Monitor, five times as many people in the USA compared with the UK have acted as business angels and invested in start-up companies. In this country less than 1 per cent of the adult population has been an 'angel'. Also the £500 million invested in this way is dwarfed by the $27 billion a year invested by US angels.

The UK's minister for women, Baroness Jay, points out that more than nine million businesses in the USA are owned and run by women. If we could just match this 'lively' situation with women entrepreneurs of our own 'we could double the number of start-up businesses in our economy', she says.

With 'new economy' businesses taking off and some new tax breaks to encourage potential angels the profile of typical backers is shifting from being predominantly male and 45 to 65 years old to include younger angels and more women. But the point is that the UK has a long way to go to match the US culture which encourages far more women to start on the road to business leadership.

Ann Iverson's story illustrates how American women can hit the heights of the business world on both sides of the Atlantic. She first arrived in Britain in 1990 after reaching the top in Bloomingdales, the world-famous New York department store. Iverson then joined the Storehouse group and rose to become managing director of the Mothercare chain and built a reputation for trying to turn around that business and the group's other struggling chain, British Home Stores. Then in the mid-1990s she joined Laura Ashley as a non-executive director. In 1995, after a succession of bosses failed, she hit the jackpot as she was made chief executive, hailed as a saviour of the declining Laura Ashley company and paid a package stretching to millions based on her past reputation and hopes that she could pull the fabrics group out of the mire. These hopes were dashed as Ann Iverson herself was forced to quit in 1997 and Laura Ashley continued to lose money. This showed that American business leaders don't always succeed. Nevertheless, Ann Iverson has interesting experience of what it is like for a woman to make it to the top in the UK.

Iverson's past as a one-time rodeo rider, born in Michigan, and with four marriages behind her and a 'shoot from the hip' attitude, singled her out from the crowd. She remembers being surprised by the prevailing different culture in Britain. 'There wasn't a well to draw from in the same way and so women don't have the same chance to reach the top', she said when she arrived. And even after she was ousted she said 'it is good to talk about this interesting subject because the issues are just as real'.

♀

Asked about the different attitudes she says: 'Women in the UK are as committed as their male counterparts, but the desire and ambition to reach the top has not been at the front of their minds. In the USA you can push a little harder. It's not so unusual to be assertive and brutally frank in the USA. In the UK it may be perceived as un-ladylike and women are geared more towards the family. That's no criticism. It is a cultural difference.'

Indeed it may be the brash, bold and ambitious side of Iverson that contributed to her downfall. Laura Ashley was after all a quintessentially English brand. Starting in women's clothes it expanded into wallpaper, fabrics and paint, and under founder Laura and her husband Sir Bernard became a byword for expensive 'style'. Founder, Laura Ashley died in 1985, just as the business was about to join the stock market. With the benefit of hindsight it is easy to say the transition from an entrepreneurial private business to an international publicly-quoted group was never a success. Iverson, in management style, was painted 'as a workaholic control freak, quick to take umbrage when her decisions were questioned'.

What was plain was that she took decisons which back-fired. Like the ideas to expand rapidly in America, increase store sizes and promote home furnishings. She brought in a largely female senior team known from her US retailing days, but these executives started to leave within months. 'She misjudged the weakness of the business and tried to move too fast', the City said. Furthermore, Iverson had a public persona that could not have been more removed from the prim and puritanical Laura Ashley and her image of 'innocence, high standards and above all a kind of scrubbed, simple beauty'. Iverson even has a potentially fatal allergy to bees, an allergy that made wafting around English country gardens looking for floral inspiration unlikely.

Ann Iverson, in her mid-50s, also posed in *Vogue* magazine wearing just a black leather coat and saying: 'All those City guys love to think of me in black leather so I may as well live up to expectation'. Relations with Sir Bernard also broke down. Though Sir Bernard had stepped down as chairman in 1993, he still remained influential as a director and as owner of 35 per cent of the company. By the end of Iverson's two years as chief executive she described him as 'severely challenging'. But in truth, the challenge at Laura Ashley, even for this go-getting American, was too great.

♀

America's reputation as a meritocracy has meant there is less of a link between social background and who reaches the top and less interest in the educational background of its chief executives. Indeed, some of the most famous, like Dell Computer's founder Michael Dell, dropped out from university.

By contrast, a survey by Hemmington Scott of 5,000 UK directors in 1997 showed, of those that went to university, 53 per cent went to either Cambridge or Oxford. Also nearly half, 48 per cent, were members of two of the best known clubs in the land, the MCC and the Royal Automobile Club. We will see later how the club network has helped men command positions in UK boardrooms.

Interestingly, Catalyst, the US social research organisation, has shown that senior women in the UK and Canada are more likely than their US counterparts to upgrade educational credentials with post-graduate degrees. US women are considerably more likely to have used the tactic of 'seeking out difficult and highly-visible jobs as a career advancement strategy'.

Despite a more meritocratic perception in the USA, there are two hotbed arenas for American executives to launch their career paths to the top. Increasingly McKinsey-trained management consultants come to the fore. But it is the so-called Ivy League graduates and MBA degree holders that have consistently hit the big time.

♀

When British Airways launched its new low-cost airline 'Go' in 1997, the choice of Barbara Cassani as chief executive shook the airline world.

Barbara, a 'sassy Bostonian who is so American she could have walked off the set of *Friends*', not only became the world's first female airline boss but did so at a very British institution.

The story of Barbara's appointment began when, while already working for BA, she answered an advert in the *Sunday Times* that read: 'Market Challenger; service industry company looking for a market challenger'.

From an initial degree in her home state of Massachusetts she got a scholarship to Princeton to study public affairs. It was there she met her English investment banker husband. She is a fan of good English and fights against American 'airline-speak' such as saying de-planing when you get off.

Barbara, after starting her career as a management consultant in Washington, then left for Britain to work for Coopers & Lybrand in London. She found consulting for companies like Kodak, Bowater and Westinghouse frustrating because she would be thinking up ideas and solutions but never would be around to put them into place.

Then, aged 27, Cassani joined British Airways in the year it was privatised by the Thatcher government, 1987. Within a few years she was experiencing working for BA at the most infamous time in its history. She had a role running a sales team in the notorious 'Dirty Tricks' affair when BA took confidential information from leading rivals like Virgin and used it to poach customers. Also, in 1990 the Gulf War temporarily destroyed the air travel market.

Barbara says she was lucky that privatisation of BA meant the airline was keen to shake off its inefficient, crusty, civil-service dominated image of state-owned days. She has been described as 'a breath of fresh air in the sometimes stuffy confines of British corporate leadership'. Also, deregulation of the airline industry in Europe had allowed new carriers to be established in much the same way as they had done in America. Not being a grey man in a suit helped her: 'I think it was an advantage to be an American woman because they saw me as something different.'

After ten years of rapid progression up the BA ranks, Cassani, was instrumental in pursuading BA to enter the fray of the no-frills, cheap ticket market in competition with a Easyjet, Virgin Express and Ryan. BA launched 'Go' with a £25 million start-up hand-out that had its rivals fuming. 'I was dying to do something where I really put myself on the line. I think I was really fed up with just being a big-company person, where if I was run over by a bus tomorrow, it wouldn't really make any difference', Barbara said about her appointment as the new airline's boss.

♀

BA's then chief executive, Bob Ayling, said Cassani impressed because of her: 'Energy, her strong intelligence, her motivational skills and ambition'. Cassani also has 'no fear in telling you what is what'.

Barbara says about her part in the strategy behind the new airline: 'They chose me because I would tell them if it was a crappy business to get into. And they knew I wouldn't do it if it was.' Ayling's comments show how the 'upfront' and 'straight-talking' characteristics that are often first nature to Americans are now seen as qualities sought after in British business leaders.

Barbara was the product of an Italian-American father who was a lab equipment salesman, and an 'unembarrassable' Irish mother who could talk to anyone. It was like an immigrant background where hard work was the family motif. 'Work really hard, go to an Ivy League school, make lots of money – it's much more of a pattern there than here', Barbara says.

Being an American manager in the UK helps, in her view, because she can laugh with the Brits but she can also ignore all that subtle social stuff about accent and schools.

In her management style, keeping staff informed is one of her trademarks. 'There are a lot of really crummy managers out there who try and manage through fear and obfuscation. That's dumb. If your role is leader then you should help people to understand things when they are complicated and try and simplify things.'

Cassani's personality is bubbly with a steely interior. This helps in trying to create the new business with a whole new culture in comparison to its parent company, but also a new business that has to be highly competitive and one that uses price as its main weapon. She is determined and capable of putting a positive spin on things. This even stretches to the 12-hour days spent on her 'third baby' that mean she rarely sees her two real young children. 'Some children are very children and dependent. My children are very cheerful and independent', she claimed on their behalf. About the personal sacrifices she has said: 'I would now be much clearer about the personal sacrifice and the amount of energy and resource that is required but I actually think the naivety is what enables you to achieve big things'.

Barbara Cassani has even been tipped to one day take over as the chief executive of the whole of British Airways. During 2000, there were also rumours that she wants to lead 'Go' to an independent existence with a stock market quote of its own. Barbara Cassani confirmed that she was getting 'itchy feet' by heading discussions on management buy-out plans with the venture capital firm Electra Partners. British Airways looked over several options and was thought to be wanting up to £200 million for its low-frills 'Go' airline. Currently, in Barbara's opinion, the airline is at a 'frustrating stage' when it is still losing money and Barbara says her options for the company will increase when it starts to make money in the third year.

♀

One of the bright, young stars of corporate life in America is Joy Covey. At 36 she has become the chief strategic officer at the online bookselling giant Amazon.co. Covey, who has an IQ of 173, is typical of those who used a Harvard MBA as a launchpad to reach the top in business.

The boss woman culture in the USA has also long been apparent in the vast privately-owned corporations. Marilyn Carlson Nelson, as chief executive of the Carlson world-wide hospitality and travel empire, is responsible for one of the largest privately-owned companies in the world. This takes in Carlson Wagonlit, a 50 per cent share of the Thomas Cook tour company and a string of hotel deals, most notably Radisson. She is nowadays recognised as a worldwide business figure and also has served on the boards of oil giant Exxon, US West and on the World Travel and Tourism Council.

Marilyn has come a long way since growing up in Minnesota. Typically for a mid-western lady she says the secret of her success has been the hard work ethic. 'You stay even by working five days a week, but you get ahead by working six or seven', she says.

She studied at the Sorbonne in Paris to gain the language ability necessary for the travel business. She worked as a securities analyst for Paine Webber for two years to gain City experience. Interestingly, here she learned about how sexist City institutions can be when she was told to call herself plain M. C. Nelson on all correspondence to 'disguise her gender'.

But the most powerful woman in American business is Carly Fiorina, who in 1999 at the age of 45 was catapulted to the top at Hewlett-Packard. When Carly became chief executive at Hewlett, she commanded a $100 million signing-on package at America's thirteenth largest corporation.

The computer maker has annual sales of more than $42 billion and Carly found herself at the head of a workforce of some 83,000. HP has been an amazing success story since it was born out of trading from the garage of one its founders in Silicon Valley in California at the start of the chip revolution. However, it had become a slumbering giant, drastically in need of new blood to shake it out of complacency.

Carly Fiorina is undoubtedly a beneficiary of a more enlightened attitude to women at the top of the business world in America. According to the business bible *Fortune Magazine*, no fewer than 300 companies in Silicon Valley are looking for chief executive officers and male company presidents have been forced to realise that pickings are not so slim if only they include the 51 per cent of the population that is female in their searches. She is also lucky in that her husband has decided to turn his back on a successful career and become a 'house-husband' in order to ease her path to the top.

Carly is a product of Stanford University and then one of the second tier MBA schools at Maryland. What fired her path to the top was success at the Lucent Technologies business spun off from telecoms giant AT&T. The previous chief executive at Hewlett had been in the job for 33 years and Fiorina's appointment was influenced by the need for a radical change of approach. She said about being brought in at the top: 'Sometimes I think it takes an outsider to be neither frightened by the legacy nor disrespectful of it'.

'In the Internet Age, things move very, very quickly. And we have to move quickly enough to catch up with that pace. We are going to preserve the best and we've got to reinvent the rest – but we've got to get on with it in a hurry', Carly said about her task.

As is the case in the UK, the new, tech revolution has thrown up extra opportunities for women to reach the top. Meg Whitman as chief executive of her massive online auction business, E Bay, worth $18 billion before the tech-

nology stock crash is rated among the most powerful business women by Forbes and she typifies those who were
also-rans while working on the 'old economy' career path
but who are superstars in the 'new economy'.

However, in America, a success culture exists for women
in all businesses. We have already seen how the media has
been a fruitful area in Britain for high-flying women. Shelly
Lazarus, as chief executive of the world's seventh largest
advertising agency Ogilvy & Mather, is an example of how
this is also the case in the USA. Meanwhile, US business
women are also breaking new ground in industries that
were male-dominated as well, as can be seen by the rise of
Debby Hopkins to be the chief financial officer for Boeing
and to claim the title of the first woman to fly so high in
US aero industry history.

# 7

# *The Division Bell*

## Women at Westminster

Baroness Margaret Thatcher stands out as Britain's first woman Prime Minister. Her rule as the country's leader between 1979 and 1990 was inspirational in many ways. The way in which she fought and won against the trade unions' power. The way she pursued radical economic policies to turn around Britain's fortunes. The way she was an ultimate conviction politician who won three general elections and changed the political climate for ever. Also, the way she fought and won the Falklands War and was a robust defender of Britain's national identity. All this and more has been well documented.

What is interesting for this book is Margaret Thatcher's place in history as a role-model for women. Has her career provided a catalyst for change in the corridors of power at Westminster? And has there been any inspiration rubbing off from women at the top in politics to those women fighting for prominence in the business world?

The 1997 general election was historic in terms of women and Westminster.

The successful election of 120 women MPs represented the biggest ever female breakthrough to what has been dubbed 'the best gentlemen's club in the land'.

Up until now, the Commons has always been at least 90 per cent male. But suddenly, by virtually doubling the number of women MPs from the 63 of the previous Parliament, about one in five members are now women.

This breakthrough was led by the 101 new Labour women MPs in what turned out to be a landslide victory for Tony Blair's party. There are reasons for this huge advance in women members which we will look at shortly. Also, we see how women took a significant grip on senior positions in running day-to-day affairs of Parliament. But for now, it is worth looking at the long struggle women have had to get this far.

The position of Baroness Jay, in the Cabinet as House of Lords leader and Minister for Women, represents a big leap forward from the days of the suffragette movement and the days when women were not even allowed to vote.

Christabel Pankhurst in 1917 laid the first tracks towards power by standing as the only candidate in her Women's Party in the election of the following year.

Amazing as it seems to us, when Betty Boothroyd has been 'running the House' as Speaker for eight years since 1992, women were not even allowed to listen to House of Commons debates until 1917, except by being separated behind a grille from the rest of chamber. In fact, Nancy Astor beat Pankhurst to the honour of becoming the first woman to take up a seat at Westminster when she became the first woman MP in 1919.

Throughout the 1920s to the 1940s the numbers of women candidates and members increased slowly but they were always heavily outnumbered by their male counterparts. Indeed, in these years, despite being heavily outnumbered in Parliament, women did not 'club together' for solidarity. And hostility led by the strident anti-feminist MP the Duchess of Atholl, elected in 1923, meant there was no common agreement to fight for women's issues.

The post-war general election did represent the first minor step-change in the history of women at Westminster.

With women making up some 5 per cent of all candidates, 24 were successful in winning seats out of a House of Commons of 615.

During the 1950s, 1960s and 1970s, women's progress at Westminster ebbed and flowed, a low point being the slump to 17 MPs in 1951 with 29 successful in 1964 providing something of a false dawn.

This stagnation at the bottom rung of the political career tree was mirrored in the fact that only a handful of women ever made it to cabinet rank. Barbara Castle was a leading figure in the Harold Wilson era of the 1960s. Although she saw herself 'as an MP first, not as a woman MP' she did admit that she herself was only able to start out on her political career due to positive discrimination in her local constituency.

Both Labour and Conservative cabinets continued to have a smattering of women around the table, but very rarely more than one at any one time.

When Margaret Thatcher was elected leader of the Conservatives in 1975 it was 'a bolt from the blue', a breakthrough that has not been repeated in either major party since. However, Margaret Beckett was elected deputy leader of the Labour Party from 1992 to 1994 and we can only speculate how much Beckett owed to Thatcher breaking new ground in the 1970s.

It is open to debate whether or not those reaching cabinet rank did so by keeping feminine credentials suppressed, or by using their gender for their advantage.

Barbara Castle, when she was a Labour cabinet minister and opposition front bench member in the 1960s and 1970s, was said to have sex appeal and a chemistry that allowed her to be in favour with leader Harold Wilson in a way that senior male colleagues could not be. She denied being aware of possessing any such appeal, though she has said; 'I always like to look my best. I think it is the duty of women, when they are in public life, to cheer up the scene to the best of their ability.'

Margaret Thatcher herself said on the eve of the 1979 election; 'I did not get here by being stridently female'. However, ministers and those who worked under her in her days in power have no doubt she used sex appeal to her advantage. Former Tory MP Teresa Gorman says Thatcher did 'flirt'. 'If you looked at her behaviour in the lobby when some of the men who were part of her inner circle were with her, like the Tebbits and Parkinsons, her manner and body language were quite different.' Gorman also remembers how Thatcher used this sexual chemistry to good effect when dealing with world leaders and winning deals on the country's behalf. In particular, President Gorbachev. 'She was quite clearly besotted with Gorbachev. When he came over to make his historic speech to the House of Commons, she looked twenty years younger. Her hair looked brighter and different and her eyes sparkled', Gorman said. Margaret Thatcher, for her part famously said of the Russian President: 'He is a man with whom I could do business'.

And a decade and a half after Thatcher's social revolution, a whole new batch of entrepreneurial women is emerging. For it was Margaret Thatcher's reforms of the business climate in the mid-1980s that led to Britain shrugging off its reliance on heavy industry. In place of this came an economy dominated by service companies. To start with, male entrepreneurs led the way, but those women who were at an impressionable age when Thatcher was in power are now shining through. For instance, in a recent *Mail on Sunday* survey of the country's richest women there were no less than 64 who earned £1 million or more a year.

Following the October 1974 election the number of women MPs was still stagnating at 27, but the quality of those that did make it to the House was high. This, alongside the move in the 1990s to fix shortlists in favour of women, laid the foundations for the situation today. In 1988 the Labour Party adopted a policy of compulsorily reserving places on shortlists for women. The next year the party went a stage further by fixing elections to its shadow cabinet by making members vote for at least three women.

By the time of the 1992 election more and more women had entered the fray with some 366 candidates. Pressure built, from campaigners like the 300 Group, to aim ambitiously high and try to get women into the Commons in equal numbers to men.

The Labour conference of 1993 took the radical step of approving 'all-women' election shortlists and thus ensuring that a much higher number of women would become MPs. In trying to secure 'a quantum leap' in women MPs, half of the Labour candidates in each region were to be selected from women-only shortlists in seats where the sitting MP was retiring.

In the years between 1993 and 1996 the Labour Party selected 132 women candidates, with 35 of these coming from all-women shortlists. The policy survived until it was challenged under Sex Discrimination Act laws in an Industrial Tribunal in 1996.

Women only shortlists were held to contravene the law and the Labour Party backed down because it wanted to avoid bad publicity in the run-up to the May 1997 election.

♀

Following the record entry of women into Parliament in 1997, many were younger MPs than had been the case in the past – the so-called 'Blair Babes'. But is also true the variety of backgrounds has diversified to reflect a more genuine cross-section of the population.

The Prime Minister was duty bound to reflect the upsurge in talented women in the Commons. So Westminster's power structure did have a very feminine feel. At one stage five women sat at the Cabinet table and the fact that the

House was one-fifth female was reflected by 30 women taking ministerial positions in the government as a whole.

At Westminster, since the 1997 election, MPs are finding that women are the management. For several years, the Speaker, the Leaders of both the House of Commons and the Lords and the Government Chief Whip were all women.

For Betty Boothroyd, becoming Speaker in 1992 capped a long Parliamentary career of her own which was preceded by 17 years of trying to fight 'unwinnable seats' to become an MP in the first place. The choosing of Boothroyd as Speaker was hailed as a major symbolic breakthrough by Margaret Beckett, who was then deputy Labour leader. 'There must be more women in key positions of authority to act as role models for others. It is of immense importance to have secured the election of Betty Boothroyd', Beckett said.

Margaret Beckett had previously fought for the leadership of the party and been a senior minister as Trade Secretary before she was made the Leader of the House of Commons in Tony Blair's government. She remembers the impact Margaret Thatcher had in turning the house into 'a much more confrontational chamber'.

Ann Taylor's promotion to Chief Whip after being Leader of the House followed a lifetime passion for politics as she became a Labour Party member when she was 14 and first became an MP at just 27. She and Margaret Beckett hoped to use their positions to influence a change in atmosphere in the chamber.

Baroness Jay has, as it were, been born for a political career since she is the daughter of former Prime Minister Jim Callaghan. The Leader of the House of Lords had also had ample experience of life in the spotlight and in high society for she was married to Peter Jay, who was made Ambassador to the USA by his father-in-law PM. Peter Jay was also an economics editor of *The Times* and, later on, at the BBC.

The handful of women in the Cabinet was completed by Mo Mowlam, who served first as Northern Ireland Secretary and then in a more roving brief as Cabinet Office minister, and by Clare Short who was made International Development Secretary.

Mo Mowlam has built the reputation as being the most influential and respected senior politician of the five of them. More than that, in the eyes of the public, she has been the most popular cabinet minister of them all, man or woman. Mowlam, MP for Redcar, says her political career was inspired by her teachers at her comprehensive school, where she was head girl. A certain Miss Morlcy was important and made Mowlam think, analyse, discuss and debate; all the skills necessary in politics. 'She inspired me and said "You can do what you want. Go for it. If you work hard, you can get there"', Mowlam recalls.

Mo Mowlam first came into prominence as a shadow minister when she was given the role of leading a 'charm offensive' to woo the City and business community under John Smith when Labour were in opposition. In the government of Tony Blair, Mowlam is known for having a warm personality and having the common touch when dealing with members of the public.

As Secretary of State for Northern Ireland she played a central role in the peace agreement reached in the province. Mo Mowlam was eventually ousted from the high-profile Northern Ireland position amidst allegations of feuding and whispering campaigns by Peter Mandelson. That her demise is also blamed on the PM's unelected civil servant Jonathan Powell, showed also how even the most popular of cabinet ministers in the eyes of the public have to fight survival battles with colleagues and the PM's 'inner circle'. Mowlam also made it quite clear she was not happy to be 'reshuffled' in 1999 to the Cabinet Office.

Here, her roles included being put in charge of a campaign to 'Banish the Bumpf'. With the added piles of 'red tape' since the last election costing business more than

£5 billion, Britain's entrepreneurial community is far from satisfied. Cabinet Office head, Mo Mowlam claimed her Banish the Bumpf campaign shows: 'A whole new approach to cut unnecessary burdens of red tape, administration and form-filling that can make life hell for small businesses and many in the public sector. . . . A lot of progress has been made, but getting regulation right means a culture change across the whole of government', she said on taking on her latest role.

Tory shadow minister Angela Browning said: 'The government's latest attempt to reduce the burden of regulation is too little, too late'. Red tape has been heaped up in many areas. The biggest bugbears are the Working Time Directive coming from Europe and minimum wage laws. On top of this, the government is making bosses more and more responsible for administering the welfare system and for tax collecting. For example, in the areas of stakeholders' pensions, statutory maternity benefit and working-family tax credits. The opposition says added red tape has cost £5.4 billion since 1997. Also, that the government has deliberately dumped the cost of employment and benefits policies on to the shoulders of business.

Mo Mowlam in the Cabinet Office role was also given the job of overseeing the government's anti-drugs campaign. By the autumn of 2000, she had become disenchanted with life in the Blair government and took the decision to stand down from the Cabinet at the relatively young age of 50. Mo Mowlam had always had a style of her own. Former deputy leader Lord Hattersley remarked about her decision to quit: 'A government can afford one Mo Mowlam. A Cabinet entirely composed of them would be a disaster.' But long-term friend and Labour MP Gwyneth Dunwoody was more charitable and said: 'It makes you think that someone at the top is afraid of powerful women'.

♀

Respected lobby journalist and political editor of the *Guardian*, Michael White, says about Tony Blair's 'top babes':

One of the complaints levied against him as Prime Minister is that most of his Cabinet women have been given what can be summed up as 'housekeeping jobs'.

Baroness Jay belongs to a generation of Labour politicians who might have made it as an MP had the dice been loaded in favour of women's selection earlier than it was.

She is a symbol, as a daughter of a former Prime Minister, of those who have been helped by patronage. Also this is a source of some of the resentment felt towards her in the House of Lords because it is she, as Lords leader, who presides over kicking out hereditary Peers.

She is not the most important woman politician of her age by any means.

Baroness Jay also courted controversy by condemning private education – while sending her own children to fee-paying schools.

'Mo Mowlam was liked and respected as a person, even by those who did not always respect her views. She achieved a lot in Northern Ireland', Michael White said.

'Margaret Beckett was among those who lost power due to a personality clash with Chancellor Gordon Brown. Clare Short had strong and distinctive views and at least she had a "proper" department to run in Overseas Development. She and Mo Mowlam are similar in that they spoke their minds. Perhaps one thing you can recognise is that women at the top are more prone to wear their hearts on ther sleeves than the men', the political editor added.

♀

The situation at Westminster puts into focus the relative failure of women, to date, to reach the top in the other major arena of influence – the business world.

Lady Howe, with deep involvement in both worlds, is probably the best qualified person to comment on what is going on. She is well known as the wife of Geoffrey Howe – the former deputy Prime Minister, Foreign Secretary and Chancellor of the Exchequer to Baroness Margaret Thatcher. But this disguises the fact she is a formidable and important figure in her own right.

For decades Elspeth Howe has been at the forefront of campaigns for equality for women. This began with the Equal Opportunities Commission. Then in 1990 she chaired the Hansard Commission on 'Women at the Top' with the brief to 'identify barriers to the appointment of women to senior occupational positions, and to other positions of power and influence, and to make recommendations as to how these barriers could be overcome.' Until 1999 she led Opportunity Now, which campaigns for women in the workforce on the grounds it makes *commercial sense* for all types of businesses. Lady Howe handed over the chair of Opportunity Now to Clara Freeman, but she still had other public lives. These included being Chair of the Broadcasting Standards Commission, President of UNICEF in the UK and governor of the LSE.

'We are at a springboard stage', says Lady Howe. Latest research shows that the number of women directors in the 200 biggest companies in Britain has doubled in the last five years. But, and what a 'but' it is, this still means they hold only 5 per cent of the directorships. Lady Howe points to the USA for comparison where one in ten top directors are women.

'It was a huge boost to see 101 women Labour MPs elected. The Tories were more disappointing, but this largely reflected the 1997 election result. What is clear is women are able, though there is still a cultural blockage', says Lady Howe.

The Opportunity Now initiative began in 1991 with the aim of increasing the quality and quantity of women's participation in the workforce, at all levels and based on ability. Prime Minister of the time, John Major, described it as: 'Undoubtedly, the boldest corporate equal opportunities initiative we have seen yet'.

When Lady Howe's Hansard Society Commission on 'Women at the Top' published its findings in 1990 it had good and bad news. It said: 'Women's representation in management has slowly increased in the past two decades, but women at the very top are scarcely visible'.

In the Civil Service, the scarcity of women at the top was equally acute, with, in the late 1980s, only 2 per cent of appointments as departmental chiefs at Permanent Secretary level being women. By the late 1990s there had been little improvement, with women taking 6 per cent of the very top positions, even though the Civil Service set itself a target of 15 per cent of women in top grades by the year 2000.

However, changing attitudes to selection procedures, and new ideas, like the introduction of 'long term special leave' which will help women and men take career breaks and then resume in the civil service, offer hope for equality going into the twenty-first century.

This change of climate has started to manifest itself in the way women took some of the most high-profile, challenging and influential public appointments during the 1990s. Former Treasury economist and business entrepreneur Clare Spottiswoode headed a new breed when in 1993 she became the mum who in some way had her finger on all the gas buttons in the country when she was made Director General of OFGAS, the UK's gas regulation body. Spottiswoode had all the intellectual credentials after studying at Cambridge and Yale and an obvious business flair after, at different times, starting up and running a giftware and then a microcomputer software company. 'Being at the top has its positives and its negatives. You have to be strong enough to take the brickbats as well as the applause', she says. But many capable women like her would not have been advanced in public life in the past until a change in attitude developed to try to make 50 per cent of all top public appointments open to women.

Significant as the big increase in the number of women successfully elected to Westminster in 1997 was, this breakthrough needs to be put in context.

The Hansard Commission showed that Britain had been coming nearly bottom in the list of European democracies in terms of representation for women. For instance, in 1990, Sweden had 133 women MPs, 38 per cent of its Parliament. Norway, Finland and Denmark all had more than 30 per cent, Germany and Italy had double the number of women MPs in Britain. Only France, with 5.8 per cent compared with our own 6.3 per cent of women making up the main chamber, fared quite as badly as Britain. Furthermore, when considering how successful women were at gaining cabinet rank, the position of all European countries was better than in Britain.

Hansard called the under-representation of women 'chronic' and said under-representation varies between different societies 'but on any reckoning Britain comes close to bottom of the league tables of modern democracies'.

So, what does this mean?

Hansard put its finger on it by pointing out that: 'Equality between men and women in the public realm is more than a matter of fairness for individuals. The decisions taken by public people have consequences for all members of society – male and female, young and old.'

The country fails to benefit from the talents and experiences of women. 'As Britain becomes an increasingly complex place in which to live, the need to make use of all available human resources grows apace. This need will not be satisfied unless women take their full place beside men in government and in opposition', the Hansard Commission said.

Lady Howe's commission also made interesting obser-
vations on why women had been struggling to get any grip
on power and influence through Parliament. There was an
unfortunate cross-fertilisation between the relatively poor
performance of women in all other fields of society and
other professions. Selection boards would be accustomed
to not seeing women present themselves after a first career
that had taken them to near the top in business, or law,
and the 'lack of appropriate background' could be used as
an excuse for not choosing a woman candidate.

Also, being an MP is holding a very visible form of power.
Femininity and power are often seen as incompatible.
'Women tend to be socialised to put themselves last and
others first, and although commendable behaviour in the
home, this attribute is unlikely to get women into the
House!', Hansard said.

But Parliament itself has been the biggest barrier to
women. The way it works makes it unattractive for
mothers. For decades, the culture of late-night sittings, or
even all-night sittings, prevailed in Parliament.

It has been debated elsewhere that women's interests
have not been properly represented in our Parliament. But
what is of interest for this book is whether the new wave
of women at Westminster has made an impact by changing
the rules in women's favour.

Unlikely as it seems, Baroness Jay, as Leader of the Lords,
and Baroness Thatcher, as first woman PM, can be brack-
eted together as two anomalies of modern politics. When
Thatcher became PM in 1979 it was then seen as part of a
new wave of women getting into Parliament. In fact the
contrary was true, as the number of women MPs in her
successful 1979 general election actually dipped by a third
to 19. Likewise, women were not even allowed to sit in the
Lords until 1958. Hereditary principles have favoured
men. Consequently, women peers have always been far
outnumbered in the Lords in the same way as men outnumber women in the Commons.

The Hansard Commission recommended this imbalance should be corrected by fixing future creation of Life Peers, peers that owe their creation to their own status rather than merely inheritance, to include relatively more women. And from the mid-1990s onwards there has been an increasingly high proportion of women among any new Life Peers, with a third or more of modern 'honours lists' being women.

In any event, Baroness Jay was a focal point for the government's attempts at the most radical changes to the constitution in respect of the Upper House seen since before the First World War. Jay, who had joined the Labour ranks in 1992, has been labelled 'the scourge of the House of Lords'.

To try and honour a manifesto commitment, the government set out to scrap the old House of Lords and its membership which has been dominated by hereditary peers. First, former Tory cabinet minister Lord Wakeham headed a commission which had the brief to come up with new proposals for membership of the Upper House and to look at how any new second chamber should exert political influence over legislation. The government broadly agreed with the principle that a new House of Lords should be made up of a majority of members who had been appointed on the basis of their own personal careers and a second minority element of elected peers. For Baroness Jay, and the government in general, the issue of House of Lords reform proved to be much harder to implement in practice than it had been to write about in a manifesto. In 2000 to 2001 a joint committee of both Houses of Parliament was meeting to decide on Lords reform.

♀

The concept of a Minister for Women had been bubbling away since the late 1980s when the Labour Party pledged to create such a ministry when it was next elected.

The record number of women elected in 1997 was reflected by MPs like Joan Ruddock, Harriet Harman, Patricia Hewitt and Tessa Jowell all, at some stage, taking junior ministerial roles in the new department.

Tessa Jowell and Margaret Jay speak about their close personal friendship and how this helps them overcome feelings of isolation in politics. 'If you are hanging around until midnight, it's nice to have a chum to have a cup of tea with and discuss matters of high policy along with views of pashmina colours', Tessa Jowell revealed in a *Daily Telegraph* interview.

During Tony Blair's first government, the Women's Unit in Whitehall did emerge with some new policies on the climate for women in careers. We will look at some of these later.

♀

Many of the new breed of young women MPs saw Westminster as an old-fashioned gentleman's club that they were eager to change. The late nights, with the tradition of divisions, or votes on debates, starting at 10 p.m., had grown up in the nineteenth century when men would work on different careers in the day and then go to the House to use it as a club and to do a bit of democracy after a good dinner.

However, it seems a promised radical shake-up in the runnings of the Commons has not materialised. There was a success in the form of pushing through the idea of the House of Commons ending its debates at 7 p.m. on Thursdays. This, it was argued, would benefit both male and female MPs with families. Nevertheless, women MPs first elected in 1997 have had illusions shattered.

Tess Kingham, a 36-year-old Labour MP for Gloucester, announced she would stand down after just one spell in the Commons in order to spend more time with her family. Also another Labour MP, Anne Campbell, led a campaign for change and organised a petition signed by 210 colleagues calling for reforms in the House. She reckoned Tess Kingham's decision could discourage women from becoming MPs in future. 'It sends out the message that Parliament is out of touch. It's not just mothers with young children. There are quite a few men who find the hours extremely difficult', she said.

Jacqui Lait had the honour of being made the first woman to become a Conservative Whip and she strongly opposed reform of working hours for tactical reasons. 'Our Parliament is an adversarial one. It all comes down to voting tactics and use of time is a tactic. Labour's majority is so large it can ram anything through. Our only weapon is to divide and split. We have played merry hell in many ways, one of which is taking votes late at night', the opposition MP explained. Jacqui Lait is from the breed of women who have no illusions that a career at Westminster is tough. 'It's next to impossible to be an active parent and an MP. Being a member is not a career it is a way of life.' Her recipe for success is: 'Having a constitution of an ox. To be good in politics you also need to be good with people, persistent and self-confident.'

Despite promises to take a new broom to Parliament's ancient working practices, the only significant reform has been the introduction of morning sittings in the Commons on Thursdays. These allow MPs to leave by early evening and travel to their constituencies for the weekends. Another idea to help women MPs, the proposal to allow breast-feeding of babies in Parliament, was opposed by Gwyneth Dunwoody MP, a longstanding member and leading candidate to take over as the next Speaker.

Other 'Blair's Babes' have turned their back on a long term career in Parliament, with Wolverhampton SW member Jenny Jones saying she will serve only one term.

And unrest over the lack of progress was stirred further when the PM's wife Cherie Blair herself chaired a debate at the Labour conference in 2000 on accusations that her husband's government had 'failed women'. The Institute for Public Policy Research looked at criticisms that Parliament had not been modernised quickly enough and that pro-family reforms of Parliament are not rigorous enough.

The debate motion was 'A Marriage of Convenience, Has New Labour delivered for women?'. It came against a backdrop of feelings that the party failed to tackle disillusion among women voters, had a poor record on promoting a woman-friendly image and was allegedly not doing enough to get women into winnable seats. Cherie Blair's involvement was welcomed by Anne Campbell MP who said: 'It will make the debate very high profile, which is just what is needed, people need to see how important this is'. But Cherie Blair's stance also fuelled criticism from those who said the PM's wife was taking an inappropriate and overtly political role.

No matter, evidence from selection boards and from those women MPs already declared as standing down suggested the number of women MPs will fall from the 1997 highs. Also, there have been suggestions that the Whitehall Women's Unit could be scrapped and replaced by an organisation that represents both males and females who have been discriminated against on grounds of gender. Meanwhile, Baroness Jay has already said she will stand down when the 2001 election is called. There are those who question whether her Minister for Women role will survive into the next Parliament.

In respect of the House of Commons itself, the introduction of a Minister for Women is proving to be more spin than substance.

♀

Baroness Jay is a woman who has played a full part in the Jay family's colourful past and is a person that many either respect or loathe. As Margaret Callaghan she met at Oxford University, and married, Peter Jay, who himself was the son of Labour politician Douglas Jay. When the couple went to Washington when Peter Jay was Ambassador to the USA in the late 1970s, Margaret caused an outrage by having an affair with the famous Watergate reporter Carl Bernstein. Peter Jay himself later had an affair with the nanny, divorced Margaret and, as part of the settlement, paid for the private schooling for their children.

As Minister for Women, Baroness Jay made attempts to preach the business case for a balanced workforce, including a balance at director level. When meeting senior industrialists, she tries to argue for equality as a mainstream business issue 'and not just a family-friendly issue'.

The most striking work in her Whitehall Women's Unit has been in quantifying the cost of being a woman in the world of work. This 'female forfeit' means that a typical woman forgoes almost a quarter of a million pounds over a working lifetime simply by being female, the unit says.

To take a couple of examples: The difference between the lifetime earnings of an average low-skilled mother of two and a working man is about £482,000. The 'female forfeit' for average higher skilled women with degrees and professional qualifications is £163,000, says the Women's Unit.

This represents a 'heavy economic price just for being female'. While celebrating some progress for women in the workplace this 'starkly underlines there are still many barriers to be overcome'.

The government has moved to close this 'female forfeit'. First, new National Minimum Wage laws gave 1.3 million an immediate pay rise. Further tax, welfare and benefit reforms meant the average working mother could claim back £65,000 of the financial gap, the Women's Ministry said.

Other measures include the introduction of Working Families Tax Credit which has the effect of guaranteeing the low-paid a minimum income of £190 a week. Also new 10p tax rates halved the tax paid by one million women, the government claimed. There has also been a very big increase in Child Benefit rates and the setting up of a national Childcare Strategy with the aim of providing one million new nursery places. These policies aim to make it easier for mothers to work.

The Women's Ministry sees the role of women in work becoming more important as trends for a more knowledge-based and service industry economy escalate.

It predicts 1.7 million new jobs created in the service sector over the next decade and of these 1.3 million will be taken by women. It is with this in mind, Women's Ministers have set themselves an avowedly political aim of improving the climate for working women still further.

Also, the ministry aims to influence the way people are selected to be the 'great and good'. 'To show that we don't ask others to do what we are not willing to do for ourselves, we are leading the way on public appointments by aiming to ensure that 50 per cent are filled by women', says Jay.

Baroness Jay recognises that women have changed their attitudes to work over the last few decades. For instance, the number of young mothers at work has doubled since 1975 and it is now just as common as not for young women to work. 'The economy has changed hugely over the last 25 years. Most women are now in work – and because they want to be and not just because they can't afford not to be', she says.

The government says it believes in successful businesses and it says it is increasingly apparent that women employees are prepared to give a greater level of commitment and loyalty than before.

'The UK needs to be able to recruit and retain the best available people from the biggest available pool and utilise the talents of all', she tells business.

On the specifics of the business case for women in the workforce, she believes that family-friendly employers benefit from reduced absenteeism and improved retention of key staff. On the wider business case, she says a diverse top team helps a company to deal better with a rapidly changing environment and a top team including women gives a business a better understanding of its marketplace.

In late 2000, the Women's Ministers spent more than £100,000 on government backing for a new magazine called *Voices* aimed at advising women how to lead their lives. The idea was branded a waste of tax-payers' money by Opposition spokesman Theresa May and the launch was greeted with a headline in the *Daily Mail* which described the ministers as 'Baroness Bossy and Nanny Tessa'.

♀

Previously, in February 2000, the Women's Ministry unwrapped one of the more unusual secret weapons used by government . . . a 'tool kit' of ideas born out of an experiment with top stores and the National Health Service. Big names like Asda and Tesco were told to share ideas for family-friendly policies with the NHS. 'In this case, it is business leading the way and the public sector following.' For nurses this means being given a chance to select their own hours, 'self-rostering'. Also, a say on the total hours worked in any year – the concept of annualised hours. Added into the 'tool kit' were other job-sharing ideas and the carrot of tax-free nurseries. 'Women particularly want more choice in their lives and more opportunities to maximise their potential. Good, flexible working practices are not only good for women but also good for families and good for business. Employers are increasingly realising the economic importance of policies that allow employees to balance work and home life', said Baroness Jay.

The 'tool kit' idea was billed as a way of trying to stem the outflow of trained staff from the already strapped NHS. 'Flexibility is the most important carrot to tempt us back to work after having children', nurses told the government. It is early days. We shall have to see if the idea can make business get better.

# 8

# *A Fair Hearing*

Barbara Wilding is uniquely qualified to say how Britain's police force is trying to shrug off its image as one of the worst cases of an outmoded, male bastion. You can count the women who have reached the very top in the force on the fingers of one hand. As Deputy Assistant Commissioner of the Metropolitan Police, she is one of them. As head of personnel for the Met., she was a central figure as her force unsuccessfully tried to stave off a £1 million sexual harassment claim. She also spearheaded the move to make the Met. a highly-trained force and a force where further women could come to the fore on the basis they have 'what it takes'.

Today, Barbara Wilding is one of the most important people in the lives of all our political leaders and the Royal family. For she is head of Security Protection and Intelligence. As such she leads 3,000 officers involved in security at Westminster and she is the senior officer involved in the safety of heads of state, diplomatic protection. She was also 'top cop' looking after the Queen Mother in her recent 100th birthday celebrations.

Meanwhile, Barbara Wilding's own steep rise in a 29-year career coincides with how the police force has been turning into more fertile ground for ambitious women.

Barbara has experienced two milestone years in that time.

First, incredible as it may seem, it was not until 1975 that the Met. Police abolished its structure of having separate women's and men's divisions. More about this distinction later.

The second milestone year came in 1994 when, for the first time ever, Barbara was one of three women who made it through to the 'final' of the annual police selection board for those aspiring for the very top. Previously, she remembers, these top boards of 25 or so hopefuls had never had more than one woman in any one year. Once through this intensive selection course, hopefuls gain 'chief officer' rank and are within sight of the summit with another three ranks to climb before being made head of a county force in England or Wales as a Chief Constable. Since 1994, the number of women who have reached this senior 'springboard stage' in the police has tripled. Women officers make up about 15 per cent of the police nationally.

And in 2001, England and Wales had three women Chief Constables out of 43 across the counties. Elizabeth Neville in Wiltshire, Pauline Clare in Lancashire and Jane Stichbury in Dorset.

Pauline Clare, 53, became Britain's first female Chief Constable in 1995 when she was appointed to lead a force of 5,000 and an organisation with a budget of £184 million annually. Her appointment marked 75 years of slow progress since this country had its first policewoman in 1920. Pauline says she was drawn to the police through 'a desire to do something good for her community'. There can be no doubt she proved just as courageous as any man on her rise through the ranks: 'I thoroughly enjoyed operations and the more difficult they were, the more exciting I found them.' Her tips are 'never give people cause for criticism and never wear inappropriate dress' and she said she always prepared well for each new rank she gained.

Elizabeth Neville has become head of the Wiltshire force while also being a mother and she remembers having to

Martha Lane Fox

Beverley Hodson

Belinda Earl
*Photograph by Panther Imaging*

Denise Kingsmill
*Photograph by Andy Lane*

Gail Rebuck

Fiona Price

Jan Hall
*Photograph © John Timbers*

Lesley MacDonagh

Anita Roddick OBE
*Photograph © Sean McNenemy
(April 2000)*

Clara Freeman

Kate Bleasdale
*Photograph by UPPA*

Kate Swann

Dame Barbara Mills QC

Rachael Heyhoe Flint

*Photograph ©*
*Philip Brown*

Lesley Smith

Lucy Marcus

Barbara Wilding

Hazel Moore

react to hostility to women in the force. Neville, when she returned from maternity leave, had been told by her Chief Super. that he thought it was wrong of her to go on working with a baby. 'That really angered me and I told him so', said Elizabeth and she was determined to go higher in the force.

For Jane Stichbury joining the Met. as a graduate entry in 1977 proved something of a fast track. But Jane, now 44, remembers a police culture 'much more male-dominated than it is now'. Ambitious women of her generation 'felt like pioneers'. Jane says she would not turn down the chance to be head cop at the Met. if ever the post was offered. 'There was a lot of teasing, a few exchanges, but we just got on with it. These days we realise people should not have to go into work feeling as if they have got to do battle', she says.

♀

Because of the vast size of the Met. force, at 25,500 police officers and 12,000 other staff, in comparison to the few thousands typical in the counties, Barbara Wilding's rank is equivalent to being a Deputy Chief Constable and she herself could clearly be in line for the very top of a police force some day.

The secret behind Barbara's rise to the top is a passion for the job. This passion involves a determination to stand up for the vulnerable in society. It is also a passion to 'put away the bad guy'. Barbara describes it as: 'A passion to do everything legal to put away the bad guy. They must not be allowed to win because of cost-cutting exercises or an over-emphasis on governmental targets that move resources away from serious crime. . . . It is important to focus on the need to do everything to win the case.'

She recalls from her time on the streets: 'I've looked into the eyes of a really bad person and I said to myself "I'm not letting you out on to the streets again". I've also shared with my staff my feeling of looking into the eye of a murderer and thinking handling this really bad person will be a test of our true professionalism to keep society safe from this person.'

Motivation of staff and gaining the confidence of key witnesses and victims is a vital part of a senior police officer's role, says Barbara. In this way, any top cop needs to work like any business person trying to bring the best out of those he or she deals with.

In this sense Barbara identifies with Inspector Morse and the Jack Frost type of detectives who built up such cult followings among television viewers. In them we loved their total dedication and moments of intuition built up from years of experience on the beat. Their eccentricity and foibles. That was part of the entertainment.

No one meeting Wilding can in any way call her eccentric. But, she does, deep down, consider all the paperwork secondary to the need to 'get the job done'. We can see in her the same kind of cop as Morse and Frost who fall foul of their officious Supers who seem more preoccupied by chasing staff reports than criminals.

'It is all very well being warm and woolly. Doing all the thank you letters etc.' Barbara does think there is too much focus on management training at the cost of operational ability.

'At the end of the day, when a jumbo jet falls out of the sky, or people are killed in a series of linked murders, you are "Top Cop". It is our operational skill that is required. We must have a vision of policing that builds a force able to combat the criminal. One that is not just focusing on the elegance of project management with a passing reference to policing.'

'We need leaders of police. Risk-takers. We need to do more policing and less politicising', says Barbara.

Her passion for the police started in her teens. Barbara grew up in Jersey. She remembers the time when she was looking for her first job in the late 1960s as a time when Jersey in the Channel Islands was starting to be flooded with cash from the mainland and elsewhere as its reputation as a tax haven began.

♀

Her first job out of school was working in one of the fashionable boutiques that had been popping up on Jersey for the first time. But that was not her. In most success stories there is an element of chance and for the police and Barbara this came when she was walking past the police HQ and saw a notice pinned up outside saying 'We need female recruits'. She applied, without even letting her parents know. At the time, she says, the police chief did everything to dissuade her. Anyhow, Miss Wilding was offered, and took, the job.

'It turned out women were in a separate unit. They really wanted a kind of glorified matron and statement-taker', she recalls. Women were only employed on statement-taking for sexual offences and as matrons for female prisoners.

Her ambition was never going to be satisfied by this. Again without her parents being in the know, Barbara said 'I had to stamp my foot down to get to the UK and to the training college'.

♀

When she did get there, she not only passed, but did so with the best marks the college had seen for five years. This was some achievement for someone who says of her own schooldays: 'they were not very happy. Although I got through all the exams, it is not a time in my life that I like to talk about.' Anyway, at school she says she 'excelled in sciences and this proved I had an analytical mind'. By passing out of the police college with flying colours WPC Wilding was on her way. But there was still one quirky little hurdle to overcome. In the early 1970s, the Met. still had a minimum height restriction of five foot four for women and five foot eight for men. The young Barbara was not 'five four', but in her own words 'they saw other qualities and let me in. Maybe they assumed I would grow some more, but I never did.' In any event, the Met. did away with minimum heights in 1975. 'Nowadays, I have come across some very good male officers who are shorter than me', Barbara says with a smile.

In 1971, when Wilding joined the Met. as a 21-year-old she joined a separate women's squad which did 'softer, less investigative work'. This involved things like sexual offences and children's cases and care cases. In 1976, just after the Met. became a more integrated force, Wilding was promoted to sergeant to lead the West End juvenile vice squad, a job she describes as being 'good fun, but depressing'.

'I studied part-time at London University. This was snatched time as it was then not seen as necessary for a young detective to be following academic study when they should be arresting people', remembers Barbara.

♀

These early days were hard graft. She worked 13 hours a day every other day, without overtime pay, 'merely for the opportunity to serve in the CID'.

'This was a very male environment. Even later on, when getting promoted to Detective Inspector, it did not get any less forgiving. On returning from maternity leave I was initially refused DI rank because no one wanted a woman DI with a brat.'

In typical combative style, Wilding issued the powers-that-be an ultimatum – 'go to court or give me a posting'.

'I was given a posting on the other side of London to where I lived. Take it or leave it I was told. I took it and have since had the pleasure of having these then senior officers involved at that time become my juniors', says Barbara.

Her first real career leap came in 1979 against the backdrop of the infamous 'Yorkshire Ripper' case. As the story of the hunt for the Ripper unfolded, so too did the picture of failings within the infrastructure of the police force at that time. In particular, the issue of a lack of a national, computerised, murder office in the UK. Wilding was transferred to HQ and was in charge, over the next four years, of introducing computers to the Met. for the first time to log crime records and to initiate the use of crime pattern information in police work.

Wilding was launched on a path that took her to the top selection board, described earlier, and to the role of being the third most important cop in the Kent force before returning to the Met. in 1998.

As head of personnel, she was well aware of the criticisms that blew up in the late 1990s of the strategic command course for aspiring chiefs at the police college in Bramshill, Hampshire. Snipers criticised the stated aim of the college to produce neither thief-takers nor social workers, but company executives. The attitudes of the Bramshill college are steeped in the jargon of business administration with candidates learning about 'managing internal and external stakeholders' as well as performance review, developing team and leadership skills and new policing philosophies and strategies. Those winning places with substantial Criminal Investigation Division backgrounds tended to be in the minority.

♀

However, the point is that the police force has changed. As Barbara Wilding puts it: 'Long gone are the days of brawn. Gone are the days when it was all about masses of male bobbies on the beat. Policing is moving into more about getting in front of a problem before it happens.' In this sense, there is no reason at all why women should not hit the top.

'Women beat for the cause, while men tend to have the attitude of being individuals within a cause', says Wilding.

So are there aspects of a woman's make-up that are particularly beneficial for police work?

'My own drive has come from a belief in the democratic process. A belief the police have to be there to protect. Each and every one of us is vulnerable at some point in our lives. It is possible that male officers will feel the same way. But I believe women have a more intuitive feel for what is needed for people to feel safe in their lives', Wilding says.

Practicalities of the job also tap 'women's skills'. 'We are being asked to do more all the time with less. Women are exceedingly good at juggling.' Wilding also believes that so-called women's skills come into play in other ways. 'We are particularly good at emergencies – at responding to the immediate situation while "keeping the home fires burning". Women are also good at constantly thinking ahead and dealing with people. Also having an affinity with the community and its pressures.'

'Women are great lateral thinkers and therefore they are good leadership material.'

While Barbara Wilding is an undoubted success story, there is clearly evidence to suggest the police has not shrugged off its 'sexist' ways entirely. During Wilding's time at the Met., the force was rocked as Sarah Locker, 38, won a compensation package for sexual and racial harassment that, including police pensions and injury board awards, could end up costing the force £1 million. Sarah Locker had become an unpopular figure in the force since winning a first claim in 1993. Her latest claim, settled eventually out of court, involved her also claiming the Met. had not learnt from the first case and not honoured anti-discrimination agreements.

'I would love to have fought her all the way in the courts. Although we considered we had a good case, I had other things to consider. It was not in the interests of either Sarah Locker, or the Met., to have a lengthy and expensive trial in the High Court on this matter. We looked at it in the round. Although we had legal advice that we could fight this case, we had to be aware that we were spending public money', said Wilding about her feelings as head of personnel.

And during 2000–2001, Scotland Yard braced itself for further sexual discrimination claims. Sergeant Belinda Sinclair claimed she felt insulted and demeaned when her superior said of her she was 'very confident . . . for a woman'. Sinclair also said that staff assessments talked of her being 'dominant and intimidating'. Now, in many people's eyes these attributes are necessary for any person to be a successful officer who has to have a tough streak to deal with tough situations, but Sinclair was trying to make the point that it was only because she was a woman that these attributes led to her being treated unfavourably. No matter about the actual rights and wrongs. Sinclair also raised the spectre of weird initiation ceremonies for women. She said that when she joined in 1983 she had the name of her home nick stamped on her breasts and that this was common practice in forces at the time. Sinclair is probably a symbol for deep-seated resentment about improper treatment going back decades in the force. Since the early 1990s, steps have been taken to end sexism, but it remains a worry that it is still ingrained.

♀

In summer 2000, Barbara Wilding received further recognition for her status in the force when a completely new post was created and she was the one given the role. Barbara became head of all Intelligence for the Met. and alongside this was put in charge of all royalty and diplomatic protection. Now Wilding is rewarded well, with a salary of £94,000. She explains that all very senior officers in the Met. get top whack and the top of the national pay scales because of the extra demands of policing the Capital and the national and international functions carried out by Scotland Yard. She also needs to have a head for figures, because she controls a £150 million annual budget.

In her latest role, Barbara Wilding says it is essential that she has had a strong operational policing background that has given her experience 'in covert operations, intelligence, in fact, the full range of activity'.

The great day of the Queen Mother's 100th birthday celebrations, 4 August 2000, was one on which Barbara was never 'off duty, or off guard'.

'I had to make sure I didn't take my eye off the ball. The day itself started with terrorist activity on the railway in West London and continued with many hoax calls.

It was a day of a hectic round of meetings necessary to ensure all the strands were brought together to keep the public safe and a celebration for the Queen Mum was enjoyed by everyone.'

Her job means she has to be prepared to put in very long days, very often. One eye has to be kept open for terrorist activity incidents which 'are all too frequent'.

'In my job, I have to be constantly on guard for any event that could, like the rocket attack on the spy HQ, MI6, affect the countless ceremonies that take place in London. We must ensure disruption is minimal and the terrorists do not win', Barbara says with conviction.

While the prolonged series of celebrations made the headlines, in police terms, Barbara's involvement in creating a whole new culture at the Met. is going to be a far more significant event.

'Part of my job is to turn the whole force into an intelligence-led force', says Barbara. This, she explains, means doing away with the old image of the model of an 'omni-competent' constable. During her time as head of personnel she identified 744 different police job titles and specifications within the Met. She initiated a 'competence framework' for every role in the force. This meant people will in future be recruited and trained in a much more specific and scientific way. 'We want to play into people's strengths.'

So, in future, will there be roles where science tells you that only women should apply? 'Unlikely, as it is about individuals, their strengths, aptitudes and abilities and not their gender. But, it could happen', Barbara Wilding replied.

She has a family. 'I could just stay at home.' Indeed Barbara and her husband teamed up to claim a nice slot in 'gong history'.

'When my husband, Jeff, and I were awarded the Queen's Police Medal in the 2000 New Year honours list, the Queen generously offered to decorate us at the same time. It is the first time the same medal was awarded at the same time, never mind presented together in the same ceremony, for a husband and wife team', Barbara recalls with pride.

So why does she put herself through all the long hours and stress? It boils down to her commitment to the work the police do. 'I believe we have a duty to everyone. That means the old lady who has lost her purse, to the victims of the very violent criminals. I suppose in setting out on my career I said to myself "I want to make a difference".'

In the force, it is still harder to make that difference if you are a woman.

♀

By resorting to the law, women have made progress in the professional world.

Until 1919, women were barred from entering the legal profession at all. Since the first women lay magistrates were appointed in 1920 the story has been one of slow, steady progress for women in the judiciary.

In modern Britain, the Prime Minister's Wife, Cherie Blair QC, not only earns a lot more as a barrister than her husband Tony Blair, she can also claim to have made a big impact even before getting her hands on the keys to No. 10 Downing St. As a leading employment QC she is reckoned to cost over £1,500 a day in court and earn in excess of £300,000 a year. Cherie Blair read law at LSE and got the best grades in her year. 'Cherie is naturally brilliant, I have to work at everything', her husband Tony has said. She then shone in the same chambers as Derry Irvine, who became Lord Chancellor, and Tony Blair, when the future PM and Cherie were trainee barristers together.

Cherie herself once stood unsuccessfully as a Labour candidate in the marginal seat of Thanet North in Kent. The two made a pact that the first of them to win a seat would pursue the political career. Well, you know the rest.

Of course, being married to the PM keeps her name prominent, but as a barrister, she has been part of a growing band of women to take the legal route to the top.

Cherie Blair is now a high-profile barrister at the newly-established firm called Matrix. This firm, set up in early 2000, has been likened to the 'Silicon Valley of the human rights law firm world' by its friends and 'a collection of super-egos' by its detractors. It is a break from normal traditional chambers of the Inns of Court and with Blair on board is creating headlines for taking on highly political cases.

Strangely, for a firm where the wife of a Labour PM is working, Matrix is being described as very elitist and money-grabbing and certainly its barristers earn several times the national average wage.

Cherie Blair herself was the centre of a political row for her part in praising the Human Rights Act 2000. She was labelled as a mixture between Lady Macbeth and a Presidential First Lady. John Bercow, a shadow home affairs minister, accused her of 'breaking the long-standing convention that PMs' spouses do not push their own political agendas'.

The way in which Cherie Blair returned to work within 54 days of the birth of her fourth child in summer 2000 and the way she did not hold back from entering the political debate is viewed as a sign she has ambitions of her own.

The Prime Minister's wife's swift return to work was influenced by her desire to encourage others. How relevant a role-model she can be is open to doubt. It is a fact that very senior and well-paid barristers can work from home and write opinions from the kitchen table if necessary in a way that is alien to the millions of women who have to travel to work.

In her personal life, Cherie Blair tried to use her pregnancy to influence a change in attitudes. She backed the concept of paternity leave by endorsing the Finnish PM in his taking two bouts of leave by saying: 'I for one am promoting the widespread adoption of his fine example'. This threw the spotlight on to her own husband Tony when the couple became the first prime-ministerial family in the UK to have a baby in office in the modern era. Tony Blair took a kind of middle way. Perhaps in any event he did not feel confident enough in senior colleagues to totally hand over the reins of power for several weeks. In truth, the British system and style of government is not comparable to the much smaller democracy of Finland, so it was unwise and unrealistic of Cherie Blair to raise the issue.

Barristers who work with Cherie Blair say: 'She really does try to help other women, and it's not just a front'. In the legal world she campaigns for more women at the bar and is known to go to great lengths to try and get places in chambers for women she has taken a shine to.

On the one hand, Cherie acts the 'superwoman' and tries to be a role-model for all women with families and a career. On the other she is not letting her declared aim of wanting to eventually become a judge be sidetracked by a spell at Number 10.

♀

The solicitors' side of the profession has for some time reflected the fact that the female half of the country's brightest young people can hope to make it on the career ladder.

So this means the likes of Lesley MacDonagh, who has risen to head the fourth largest law firm in Europe, and Denise Kingsmill, who is one of the most influential voices in deciding on 'fair competition' in UK business, are able to stand out like beacons on the summit.

Each of them has fascinating personal stories, which we will explore in detail later. But first it is worth looking at the figures from the Law Society that serve to show how things have changed, while at the same time emphasising there is still a long way to go.

By the end of the 1980s, slightly more women than men were setting out on solicitors' careers. In 1989, there were 1,594 female hopefuls embarking on the two-year traineeship after school or after graduating, compared with 1,464 men.

A decade later, the profession as a whole had grown and opened up more opportunities with 6,056 starting training in 1999–2000. Interestingly, women entrants still outnumber men, with 3,218 women beginning legal training and 2,834 men.

When we look at the next hurdle stage, when hopefuls pass and are 'admitted to the roll', or become qualified solicitors, we see evidence of a change in the climate.

A decade ago, more men would be winning the chance to take their careers beyond the first traineeship rung. Either more men would pass, or more men would choose to continue the arduous career. But in 1998–1999, women qualified solicitors outnumbered men by 53 per cent to 47 per cent. Still some fallout from the raw material of trainee entrants, nevertheless more women making law a career.

So this gives a picture of the early days in the careers of solicitors.

What happens next? When you consider who becomes the boss in legal firms, the picture of male dominance is a familiar one, even though there is hope for the future. In 1999, male partners in firms outnumbered female partners by more than two to one. The Law Society says around 28 per cent of partners are women. On the rung below partner status at assistant partner, men are still twice as common. It is only when you get to the level below this, assistant solicitors, that women predominate and they do so by more than two to one.

♀

As head of Lovells, the fourth largest law firm in Europe, Lesley MacDonagh stands out in a position as a woman at the top of her profession. She is among a growing breed of women who have made a breakthrough to the top of law firms in the 1990s.

Lovells has grown rapidly in the last decade. The firm is based in London and has 27 locations around the world with 2,500 staff and 270 partners. 'It is an exciting time in the legal market, with a lot of consolidation going on', she says. As managing partner since 1995, Lesley, aged 48, has won plaudits for overseeing this expansion and knitting together the new people, most recently with the integration of Lovell White Durrant and the international firm, Boesebeck Droste.

Lesley has made it to the top of Lovells after being elected a partner when she was 29.

As someone who has had four children, while so obviously also having a successful career, she is an example of someone who has defied the odds. But her own story illustrates how important it is for there to be an enlightened attitude as a prerequisite for a woman to reach the top. In Lesley's case, she was actually elected as top partner while she was away on maternity leave with her third child. Admittedly, she was fortunate in having a husband, Simon McDonagh, who is also a partner at the firm. 'At least he doesn't glaze over when I discuss work issues at home', Lesley jokes. 'I never craved the position of managing partner and I was flattered when another colleague urged me to put my name forward'.

This implies that Lovells had a top team that was extremely open-minded and not beset with people out to sabotage her career. 'In my experience, the biggest hurdle was that the biggest tie of all, namely the family, was pulling me in the other direction, rather than the case being that men in the firm had an attitude against women', she recalls. In Lesley's case it also emphasises that she is someone who obviously inspires loyalty. On a personal level, this meant that Lesley's nanny for her children went through two separate bouts of maternity leave for herself and still came back to work for the top lawyer each time.

By her own admission, Lesley acknowledges the importance of being lucky. 'I cope by a combination of luck, organisation and support from my colleagues.' The MacDonaghs live ten minutes away from the Lovells HQ in the Holborn area of London and as managing partner she does remember insisting for a few key meetings while having the second half of her family to be held at her home. This illustrates how it can be easier to cope with families when you are at or near the top, rather than on the early rungs of the career ladder.

Lesley recognises the dilemma faced by women who are ambitious in their careers and who also want to have families.

'You can't underestimate the other god in your life. There is a major deterrent to be promoted and devote even more hours to sitting on even more committees in the way that is necessary to get ahead in law firms', she says. 'I still think that facing up to the twin gods of family pull -v- career pull is the big one for career women with children. Whilst you can keep (with luck and discipline) the demands for both roughly in balance, then you have a real chance of getting anywhere you want to. Physically, the pace of life for me has been fine. But, when one side goes out of balance, then the maternal responsibility generally wins and I don't think any system will change this.

What society (and men!) can do is to help women with children keep the balance as far as possible, recognising this primary pull and responsibility is nothing to do with wanting career, or work, to take second place. Women don't want to delegate everything to do with their children – they want to influence them, so the time pull is always going to be there', she believes.

Her first child, now 15, came after three years as a partner and her second six years later. 'I was lucky I had children who slept at night. If I had had screamers, being bright-eyed and bushy-tailed in time for meetings at work at 8.30 a.m. would have been impossible.' This biological luck did, she admits, mean she was not deterred from going on and having children numbers three and four.

As managing partner, Lesley is in a good position to reflect on the personal qualities that lawyers need. 'I am increasingly impressed by the achievements of female colleagues in different aspects of management and believe that a balanced female/male team brings a great deal to the corporate party,' she says.

'Women interview very well at the graduate entry stage. They show good non-legal skills.' This backs up why the Law Society figures show more women setting out on the legal career ladder than men.

'Once in the job, women are good team players and, as a generalisation, men are often more flamboyant and more concerned with point scoring in meetings. Women do have a lot to bring to the party. Women tend to be more conciliatory and consultative, and this goes down well with clients', she says.

'Being a woman is useful in helping colleagues with difficult and personal situations when I think men, in particular, would feel less inclined to "open up" to another man.

The main disadvantage is in not sharing the ingrained love of team sport, which I do think gives men a remarkable and (almost wholly) positive bond', says MacDonagh.

As managing partner of Lovells, Lesley is in charge of a business that charges around £250 million a year in fees to its clients. 'I stress, this is not a profit figure, I wish it was!' This level of fee income gives Lovells the equivalent status of a FTSE 100 company. However, Lesley is not in the same position as a top plc chairman or chief executive in terms of actually having the same power. The partnership structures of law firms means that all 250 partners of Lovells own the business between them. For Lesley, this means she has to be 'more diplomatic and collaborative' than an autocratic company boss might be. For instance, if ever there is need to replace or fire a partner or elect a new partner to the top committee then all the firm's partners have a vote and a say.

Lesley MacDonagh's experience is echoed by the managing partner at Penningtons, Lesley Lintott. Lintott was chosen as the head of the firm Penningtons in 1997 after a 25-year career with the same solicitors stretching back to when she was first articled in 1972. Penningtons is medium-sized with 48 partners, 21 of whom are based in the City, and 300 staff in all. Lintott says it is still a male-dominated profession, but the climate has opened up considerably. In 1997, she was one of only three female managing partners at leading London law firms and now there are 'ten to 15'. She also believes women have, in general, better listening skills.

'In law firms, the culture of partnership structures means everything anyone owns is still on the line. That means every partner has a say. Managing lawyers is like trying to herd cats. They tend to be individualistic in a way that wouldn't be apparent in a corporate structure', she says about her job.

So how has Lesley MacDonagh used her role to change the climate in Lovells? Lesley says she has tried to encourage the very supportive attitude she has known throughout her career with the same firm. Over 50 per cent of the qualified staff are women and she discourages any 'them and us' feelings.

She does not appear to have had any great success in altering the way her lawyers work. The incredibly long hours. The ever striving to please clients, even at week-ends. 'There is an acceptance that the rewards, in terms of high salaries, mean that long hours are inevitable.'

It is in this area we get an idea of what kind of mindset and what kind of motivation is needed to be a top lawyer, man or woman.

Lesley acknowledges the demands of the profession do mean that the people involved have to put their personal interests to one side. Nevertheless, she is intelligent, she obviously has the ability to weigh up pros and cons and, at the end of the day she would not have got to the top without wanting to be there and unless she agreed to be a contender. 'It is not realistic to ask the world to slow down. We have to satisfy clients and that means being there for them. Lawyers do need to come into the office sometimes on weekend mornings. It is often the most productive and most uninterrupted time. And actually, you do feel good about it.' This tells us that people like Lesley do get some kind of thrill out of the chase to please clients and 'do it all'.

In fact, far from getting more civilised, it seems the job is becoming harder and more competitive. 'Everybody performs to a much higher level today. The job is much more specialised and clients are much more demanding. At pitches for new business, clients are looking for a real understanding of the industry. Our big challenge is to know the client's business inside out.' At any one time, Lovells has around fifty of its staff out on secondment. In human resources terms Lesley says there is always highly-paid legal work on offer because 'the country only has a finite pool of bright and skilled people'.

What is surprising to those outside the law firm world is the absolute cut off that occurs when a leading solicitor becomes the boss.

As managing partner, Lesley no longer has the direct and total involvement described above. She obviously misses the days when she was in charge of the environmental and planning law side of her firm. 'It is a big decision to leave law behind for management', she says. By this, she means it is practically impossible to retrace your steps and go back into the day-to-day practice once you have crossed the management divide. The entrepreneur who has built his firm from scratch or the company chairman of a medium-sized plc would still reckon to want to be far more involved in the business.

When at the sharp-end, as it were, Lesley most enjoyed 'getting under the skin of people's business'. She was involved in many of the biggest public transport and environmental enquiries. This involved acting for the developers who fought for years to get Stansted Airport built.

She describes as her most 'delightful' case, when she acted for the head of Civil & Marine, one of the biggest aggregates businesses, who was challenging the building of the Dartford to Thurrock bridge crossing the Thames. She admired her client for being prepared to take his case 'all the way to the House of Lords, on principle'.

One of Lesley's roles on the Council of the Law Society means she sits on a committee for the City and the big issue is surrounding law on e-commerce transactions. Additionally, she is on the government's Property Advisory Group which assists in advising the Secretary of State for the Environment on current environmental and property issues.

She says she does not have much room in her life for external passions. But one of hers is as a leading member of the Citizenship Foundation, a body that tries to educate teachers to get across the message of how to be a good citizen in the widest sense. 'The Foundation is against anti-social behaviour and is also keen to make sure people know their rights', she said.

♀

In any list of rulers of the business world, Denise Kingsmill is up there at the very top.

Denise has used her legal career as a stepping stone to be one of the most influential voices in shaping the business landscape. As deputy head of the Competition Commission, she has ruled on the biggest City mergers and on the most headline-grabbing monopoly cases.

Kingsmill ordered the break-up of the country's leading milk producer. She led the team that looked into the British milk industry and decided that Milk Marque, which supplied about half the country's milk, had been exploiting its monopoly position to win unfair price rises, and needed to be disbanded.

Kingsmill's role at the body which took over from the Monopolies and Mergers Commission also saw her lead the investigation into British car prices and rule on the shape of Britain's cable telephone and pay-for-view television industry when NTL and Cable & Wireless joined together in this area. Currently, she is heading the investigation into the multi-billion pound takeover of Abbey National by Lloyds TSB. Also she ruled on the contracting regional newspaper industry in the UK with deals such as Mirror Group's sale of regional papers to Trinity plc. And her views affected City investment banks when she outlined ways to end monopolies in share issue underwriting.

'We are in favour of competition. Not merely anti-monopolies for the sake of it,' is how Denise describes her new job title. She has just been re-appointed for a new four-year term at the Competition Commission running until 2004. But Denise Kingsmill is a name to watch and she makes no secret she would one day like to be boss of one of the giant corporations herself.

'I have been offered the post of being chairman of a top plc, but I turned it down. I can't do both jobs at the moment. But maybe in a few years' time', she told me.

♀

Denise's rise to such an influential position is due to her own ambitious personality and due to the high profile she gained from her legal career.

About her rise in the legal world, she says: 'It felt like a fight'. An appropriate description when she came to notoriety while defending the former boxer George Walker against the board of the Brent Walker leisure company which collapsed in the 1990s under a mountain of debts. But the fight Denise went through was as much to get established in what had been a male-dominated profession.

And there is no doubt she likes being a role-model for other women achievers and that she aims high. She wants to be remembered as 'the toughest, bloody deputy chairman ever'.

Denise Kingsmill was born in New Zealand to an RAF officer father and a Welsh mother and she moved back when nine to grow up in South Wales.

Reading Economics and Anthropology at Cambridge, she remembers Cambridge in the 1960s as 'a boys' club'; 300 men to about six women and an atmosphere she did not feel part of. Contemporaries at Cambridge included Salman Rushdie and she later shared a house with him in Chelsea. Prince Charles was there 'but I can't say I moved in his circles', she says.

She went into industry for her first job in 1968 and spent the early part of her career in marketing with ICI and the International Wool Secretariat. A posting to Paris in the early 1970s impressed upon her the importance of dressing the part and she did this as a kind of duty for a woman in her profession because 'clients want me to look like a high-powered lawyer'.

♀

Denise says she remembers being disenchanted about life at the top in management in her earlier days in industry. 'At that time there was no Marjorie Scardino, no women chief executives. It was difficult to see how you could progress in business as a woman', she said.

But Denise has always stood out from the crowd. She is the kind of woman who provokes strong reactions. She has been very good at marketing herself.

A male colleague said about her in an interview for *Management Today*: 'In a male-dominated society, if you are a powerful woman who is tall, blond and attractive, it is inevitable that you are going to be treated with suspicion. Most men are simply shit-scared of her.'

Barbara Cassani, who we know is a top businesswoman in her own right, once worked alongside Kingsmill on a community heath charity board and recalls her as being 'incredibly effective at getting things done and always with incredible style and humour'.

Denise Kingsmill, in her own opinion, has gained her powerful role in industry regulation because 'they wanted someone with the legal rigour of analysis and good communication skills'.

Indeed her talents made her a candidate to become the next Director-General of the Office of Fair Trading. The civil service 'powers behind the scene' urged her to stand only then to take her off the short list and eventually appoint another man, John Vickers. The excuse given for the backstabbing that prevented her gaining a higher profile role in policing the consumer society was that she would have been a too 'spicy' choice.

About her background, Denise says getting away from the Welsh valleys 'was definitely an escape'. University contemporaries remember her in those days as being attractive, naive and red-haired. But when you speak to the high-flying Denise today there is no trace of any accent and she has turned 'striking blonde'.

Denise suggests the best thing that she did in career planning was being a stay-at-home mum to two children when she returned from Paris in the mid-1970s and at the same time studying for Bar exams. But, entering law later than most, she was astute enough to realise her best route for progression was as a solicitor. 'As a late entrant, it was important that I got on with it, didn't mess around', she says, and this led to a quick qualification period when she was 33. This 'no messing' approach is what lawyers who have worked with her attest to. When at the City law firm D. J. Freeman in the 1990s, she acted for Peter Wood, the founder of the Direct Line telephone insurance business which was taken over by Royal Bank of Scotland. 'It was very useful having her negotiating skills and presence',

Peter Wood said of Kingsmill after she had won for him a £24 million exit package. Critics translate this approach as being 'pushy and ambitious', while friends talk more of a person that has 'charisma' and the knack of getting her own way.

Before joining D. J. Freeman, Kingsmill remembers having a 'fabulous time' working as an employment law and trade union law specialist during the industrial strife of the early 1980s in Britain. In particular, she represented the ASLEF rail union in the 1981 national strike and later, in 1985, she set up her own law firm and dealt with sexual discrimination cases.

David Freeman, as senior partner until 1992, was known as a man keen to give promotion to women with potential. His daughter-in-law is Clara Freeman, who we have already written about as the leader of Opportunity Now and the first woman to make it to the board of Marks and Spencer. And Denise Kingsmill calls David Freeman 'very responsive to women' and 'the nearest thing I have had to a mentor'. Freeman for his part praises her 'very good mind'. City bankers who came up against her on the share underwriting inquiry also put a finger on what is needed to succeed in their environment by saying she is capable of getting to grips with issues very quickly.

Between 1993 and 1996 Denise dotted between another two City law firms before taking her job as deputy chairman of the old MMC. She is a Governor of the College of Law and an Honorary Fellow of the University of Wales, Cardiff. She is a non-executive Deputy Chairman of MFI Furniture Group and a director of the Norwich and Peterborough Building Society and a Trustee of the Design Museum.

Denise has been openly ambitious. She says what guides her is 'a determination to make a difference'. 'Most boards could use a healthy dose of diversity in their make-up. This would make them more dynamic and energetic', she believes.

She herself has the ability to 're-invent herself', when necessary. Kingsmill hopes to use her role to bring a greater degree of openness to the Competition Commission. But, still only in her early 50s, don't bet against another high-profile career move. 'I'd love to be a chairman of a plc, that would be an exciting thing to do', she has said.

# 9

# *Opportunity Knocks*

## Tapping the Talent?

The year 2000 could go down as the year when 'Girl Power' received the biggest boost to its credibility in Britain. This boost came from the classrooms and the graduation halls. Quite simply, girls are looking more intelligent than the boys.

For the first time, girls picked up more top grade passes than the boys in the 'A' level exams. They achieved top As in 18.1 per cent of the exams they took, while the figure for boys was 17.5 per cent, and girls also prevailed in B and C grades, leaving boys with the scant consolation of doing better in D and E grades. This greater 'A' level success has been followed through, with more than half of the brightest young people, in the shape of those going to university and higher education, being women. When looking at who is graduating in the new century, women scoop the lion's share of the top degrees. Girls got more 'first class' honours degrees than the boys for the first time ever. Figures from Britain's 170 universities and colleges revealed that girls won 11,000 'firsts' and boys 10,800, a stark reversal of the trend seen in the mid-1990s when boys scored 2,000 more top degrees than the opposite sex.

Since the GCSE exam system was introduced in 1988, girls have also outperformed boys in this set of teenage exams.

Education experts believe the shift towards coursework and away from exams as the prime assessment tool has helped women. 'Continuous and conscientious input' favours women, whereas boys could in the past score with 'flair and imagination' in a one-off exam, it is argued. The macho spin on this would be that men adopt a higher risk-taking strategy when it comes to preparing for exams, while women revise much more comprehensively. With degrees increasingly being awarded on the basis of continual assessment, rather than all or nothing finals, this is debatable.

The country's best-known scientist, Professor Susan Greenfield, says the only major difference between the brains of men and women is a difference in the 'motorway' connecting the two sides of the brain. Who knows? Perhaps, girls have been better at using what they have got.

Greenfield herself is a neuroscience fellow at Lincoln College Oxford University and by coming to the top in the academic world is something of a ground-breaker. In academia, things are fine at junior level, but then there is 'antagonism' at senior level because the men have little experience of women as top professors in the past. 'Women are often called strident, whereas men are called tough', she remarked in an interview on 'Desert Island Discs'.

The 'girls compared to boys' battle in education will go on. What does matter is whether or not the country is making best use of its most talented people.

With this in mind, research showing that women are not being rewarded equally for being the best graduates is worrying. Figures from the London School of Economics revealed that women are 50 per cent more likely to go into 'non-graduate calibre' jobs. Also, all women graduates, even those with first class degrees, are being paid salaries around 10 per cent lower on average than male graduates.

♀

The need to improve the climate for women, *because the country had not been best using their talents and because it makes commercial sense to do so*, was the spur to the creation of the Opportunity Now campaign. The campaign grew out of Lady Howe's Hansard Commission which looked at the prevailing climate for 'Women at the Top'. At that time, fewer than one in a hundred executive board-room posts were held by women. Furthermore, prospects for change were not great for the immediate generation with only one in fifteen at the tier below boards, at senior manager level, being women.

Beginning life as 'Opportunity 2000', the initiative began in 1991 with an aim of increasing the quality and quantity of women's participation in the workforce, at all levels, and based on ability. Clara Freeman took over the reins from Lady Howe in 1998 and the campaign changed its name in 1999 to 'Opportunity Now' to give it new impetus for the new millennium.

♀

When it comes to taking on stiff challenges, Clara Freeman is an expert. Not content with one hot seat, she has experience of sitting on two of them.

At Marks and Spencer she headed UK stores' personnel and corporate affairs at a time when our best-known retailer was going through 'horrendous' boardroom battles and lost the 'most profitable store' title. Furthermore, Marks and Spencer's standing in the City sank to a ten-year low and, in the opinion of some, it even became a candidate for a rescue takeover bid.

Alongside this, she continued to lead the 'Opportunity Now' campaign which is trying to kick the City out of decades of hostility to women.

Amazing as it seems, for a retailer that was the epitome of a successful British stores group, Marks appointed its first Marketing Director and only started to advertise seriously for the first time in its 115 year history in 1999. Of course, Marks also had a painful and protracted hunt for another chairman and a new chief executive after the exits of Sir Richard Greenbury and Peter Salsbury in a spell of boardroom disquiet that was described as 'a horrendous, absolutely awful period'.

Under Marks and Spencer's purges in its boardroom, a new chairman from Belgium arrived in the shape of Luc Vandevelde. He decided upon further shake-ups of job responsibilities in the top team. Clara Freeman quit Marks and Spencer, along with other senior executives. 'She took the decision herself', said a spokeswoman.

'The new person coming in was going to take a huge chunk of my responsibilities. It was a wrench to leave because I had been at Marks since the mid-1970s', Clara said.

Clara Freeman got a £270,000 pay-off on leaving Marks and she decided to stay at the helm of Opportunity Now, a campaign that believes our businesses have been losing money because they still do not make best use of half of the country's talent, namely the half that is female.

At Marks, Clara Freeman, in her personnel capacity, was in charge of 60,000 staff. About 60 per cent of the managers are women.

It is in the area of maternity that the economic case for Opportunity Now's beliefs kick in. Talking about staff retention, Clara Freeman said: 'About half of our mothers came back. I would like it to have been more. We even offered staff the option of a five-year career break, though at the end of the day it is down to personal choice.'

But Marks still suffers hugely by having to replace and retrain. Clara said: 'It costs the company £50,000 to attract, recruit and train a store manager in the first year. Of this, £18,000 to £20,000 is the salary, depending where you are in the country. So Marks wastes more than £30,000 if a manager does not come back to its stores.'

Clara Freeman took over as head of Opportunity Now from Lady Howe, who had run it since its inception in 1991. After nine years, the campaign has grown in size from 61 to over 360 organisations that range from top plcs, like Glaxo Wellcome, to the Treasury.

By the time Clara Freeman took over its leadership, Lady Howe suggested a 'springboard stage' had been reached but it was recognised something like a Bunsen burner had to be put under our boardrooms. For instance, still only 3.6 per cent of the UK's directors of public companies are women. Hence the campaign name changed to Opportunity Now in the hope of shaking complacency and sparking immediacy and action. 'We will look at the cultural barriers to women's promotion. What is needed is a culture change whereby what matters is what you produce and not just how many hours you are at your desk. We need to counter that macho emphasis on "presenteeism"', says Clara Freeman. 'We are losing out as a country because we are misusing our human resources. Half our graduates are women, but this talent does not rise to be top decision-makers in our businesses.'

Clara Freeman herself stands out. In 1996 she became the first woman on the board of Marks. This is remarkable when the vast majority of the retail staff and its customers are women. Many would say Marks' fall from grace was partly because of its male-dominated culture at the top. Its corridor of top offices has been likened to something Kafka would have invented. Communication, something women executives are better at, has been poor. Certainly, Marks' decline can be linked to a fuddy-duddy culture that contributed to it becoming way out of touch with the modern, cut-throat and fast-changing retail environment.

Tales from the bad old days suggest the management was just as concerned with preserving a hierarchical structure as with bringing the stores into the twenty-first century. For instance, the previous top management were known as 'gold top' because they had coffee served in a gold-rimmed cup while other senior management were 'silver tops' because they had to make do with silver-rimmed cups.

What did Clara think about being the lone woman top executive? 'The situation was and is not good enough. Women are still under-represented.'

So will the situation be changing? 'I hope so. At the next tier below me at the board there were three women divisional directors. When I was appointed in 1995, there was only one. That was myself.'

During 2000–2001, the upheavals at Marks continued. In the latest board reshuffle, Alison Reed was promoted to Finance Director to replace Robert Colvill.

So, why have women not been making bigger breakthroughs? 'The problem is very structured work environments at the top of large plcs. The rules and regulations of the roles make it impossible to carry out the job together with domestic roles,' she said.

Clara Freeman, 48 and married with two children, has some radical-sounding views on the way mothers are rated in the business world. 'Motherhood can develop skills in things like mediation that are highly useful. I would like to see mums highlight motherhood on their CVs and even describe the experience as "project management".'

Clara had been with Marks all her working life. She joined in 1975 as a buyer in the women's clothing department, after an MA in History from Oxford. By the early 1980s she was responsible for the first M&S range of furniture and the launch of the home furnishings catalogue. Stints in charge of gifts and then childrenswear followed before she moved upstairs to personnel in 1991.

She sees a direct link between a happier, more balanced, workforce and businesses like Marks and Spencer being able to turn the corner.

Before she quit the stores group, she was involved in trying to create a new atmosphere and image. 'We want to make it a modern and enticing place to shop. There will be real emphasis on the customer. We are using a lot more training methods to enable sales advisers to make time to serve the customer', Clara said. Amid stringent job losses and cost-cuts at head office, Marks promised to turn more back-office staff into staff actually dealing with customers on the shop floor. This means alien concepts like 'queue cruisers' and 'greeters'. Also Marks is going more contemporary in its styles. Dare one say it, even 'sexy'. It has signed up superstar designers like Katherine Hamnett and Betty Jackson who will introduce designer clothes into stores which will be more expensive than the existing main ranges and have their own dedicated floor space. Marks has also brought in the more contemporary and sexy 'Agent Provocateur' ranges and others to try to attract younger shoppers. It has also tried bringing the 'preppy', New England Brooks Bros stores to Britain. Will all this be enough to reverse a fall in sales by one fifth? We shall have to see.

Clara Freeman would appear to still have a long way to go before her other big challenge, Opportunity Now, turns into a full success. 'Equality of opportunity does not mean positive discrimination as far as I'm concerned. But the gender issue is still not cracked. There is a risk of complacency which represents a threat to the competitiveness of the UK.'

'I see a complete overlap on our aims of competitiveness in general and increased productivity coming from a more motivated workforce', she says.

But it is in the City that a more proactive Opportunity Now has its work cut out. While stopping short of 'naming and shaming' Clara Freeman wants to fill in the gaping holes. At the time of the re-launch in July 1999, only six top financial firms were members. There are flickering signs of success in the new century. For instance, the Lloyd's insurance market, long a male bastion in the City, joined Opportunity Now. Also, among Opportunity Now firms, 35 per cent of managers are women compared to just 18 per cent across the whole country.

How will she know when the campaign has got beyond the 'springboard stage'?

'My aim is to really increase the number of our organisations so that we cover the biggest proportion of all employees in the UK. We want people to work hard on a proper work/personal life balance.'

The campaign believes that business and ultimately the country, will suffer, unless organisations tap the full potential of half the population and create a culture in which both women and men can contribute.

♀

Lady Elspeth Howe has experience as a businesswoman through sitting on the board of Kingfisher, the huge retailing group with interests spanning Woolworths, the Comet electrical chain, Superdrug and B&Q. Also, she has spent several years as a non-executive director at Legal & General and United Biscuits. For a decade she has chaired the BOC Foundation for the Environment and helped run Business in the Community.

As such, she is a person who has hands-on involvement in shaping society in so many ways, I'm sure you will agree. So, when Lady Howe says: 'My instinct is that we are at a springboard stage', when asked how far along the road women have got, it is right to take notice. However, as an equal opportunities campaigner, Lady Howe has always been prepared for it to be a very long innings. 'It was never a short term aim', she says.

In the years 2000 and 2001 there was evidence of a ground-swell of women becoming directors in greater numbers. You could take notice of the broad picture. Figures from the Institute of Management show 33 per cent of all directors across the whole business spectrum are women.

Also, that an entrepreneurial culture is emerging for women. Information group, Experian, found that record numbers of women have been reaching the boardroom in small businesses. 'As service industries take an increasingly larger proportion of the UK's economic base, it is women that are leading this change', it says.

Alongside this, Lloyds TSB, with its Female Focus 2000 initiative, found that women entrepreneurs have been catching up with men and that equal numbers of successful start-ups reaching a turnover of £1 million or more were run by women as men. 'Women setting up in business are an economic force that cannot be ignored. These business start-ups will become a major contributor to the wealth of the UK, with many growing to be medium-sized enterprises that are the backbone of the economy', commented Pat Zadora, chairman of Business and Professional Women UK.

London Society of Chartered Accountants found that many companies are misusing and then losing female talent. Its survey of a random sample of 350 business start-ups in London found that 67 per cent had been established by women. Of these, seven out of ten said negative experiences in previous jobs had driven them into entrepreneurship.

Sue Birley, professor of entrepreneurship at Imperial College Management School, says the London findings represent a wider trend. 'More women are starting their own businesses as a way of developing their careers', she says. Factors driving this growth include the high divorce rate and an increase in female role-models, as well as a sense of not 'fitting'. Women are by and large much more flexible [than men]', she says. 'They may well find themselves unhappy with hierarchies and be impatient.'

♀

However, we need to search for evidence of real power. Here you will see around 6 per cent of directorships at the UK's giant top 200 companies are held by women. But the London Business School remained so concerned that progress in the business world was not matching progress made in professions like law and medicine that it launched its 'Breaking the Mould' campaign in autumn 2000.

'The entrenched patriarchal structure of the business world has been a kind of cosy club that has not made for strong corporate performance', said professor John Quelch from LBS. 'Businesses today face challenges of forming joint ventures and managing strategic partnerships. It is not about being a bull in a china shop like the old days', he says.

Elizabeth Coffey, with her study of leadership styles of 50 top female entrepreneurs, backs up this appreciation of women's skills. 'Women are much more into developing learning cultures. They'll create teams rather than divisions and hierarchies.'

We will look at whether opportunity really does knock for women. Also, at just how good the campaign's 'commercial case' is. But first, it is useful to chart just how the climate has been changing.

From Lady Howe's perspective as a campaigner of long standing and experience it is possible to stand back and take comfort in seeing that things have definitely changed. And it could be a decisive change for the better. Lady Howe acknowledges it can be misleading to focus on the bald statistics of boardroom headcounts. Or even at titles. 'How many people do you know in no higher than middle management roles in US companies that walk along with the title of Vice President', she quips. 'No, to measure progress you have to ask about *real power*. Ask whether directors have real influence or not.'

What has been encouraging to her is the emergence of women who have reached a position of pre-eminence in a previously male dominated arena ... the City and high finance.

Carol Galley has risen to become one of the most powerful people in the City, man or woman. As head of fund management group Mercury Asset Management she held the trump card that has swayed the outcome of many multi-billion pound takeover battles. For instance, when her support of Granada was decisive in its hotly-contested bid for Forte. For Lady Howe it is the profit and loss motive that has been helping women turn the corner in terms of how seriously they are taken as a force in the business world. 'The "bottom line" realisation and mentality could be the turning point', she says.

Lady Howe, aged 66, can draw on a wealth of experience of working for change in society. She has been a political animal since the 1960s. Chairing women's groups and working for the Conservative Party and campaigning for her husband when he ran as an MP until his elevation to the peerage in 1992. Aside from her equal opportunities work, she has been a Justice of the Peace and been active in legal reform on topics such as legal aid, magistrates' courts and the parole system.

It is worthwhile looking at how progress for women in business, in Lady Howe's view, has accompanied a shifting in attitudes in men. 'I don't personally approve of positive discrimination. My guiding principle has always been that companies and society should make it possible for the best people to come through', she says.

So, it is no doubt heartening for her that women are making an impact on merit and because of appreciation of the business case.

Thirty years ago, the 'Clubby Culture' prevailed. Men believed that boardrooms were their fiefdom. That it was their City. That it was their country to run. This meant men did not look beyond their circle of friends from schooldays, from sport or from their clubs to replace directors who moved on to other companies. This meant men did not know about women being available, let alone capable, of being brought in as non-executive directors. Without reaching this first rung of the ladder there was no chance of reaching the top, recalls Lady Howe.

Then in the early days, when Elspeth Howe started out at the Equal Opportunities Commission, she remembers being criticised from both sides. 'I remember thinking I was in a situation where the analogy of "Scylla and Charybdis" was so apt', she said, referring to the twin threats that Odysseus had to steer through in Greek mythology. 'On the one hand, feminists attacked our organisation as an inadequate fop. On the other, we were up against the scepticism of the male dominated unions and employers. I thought to myself that when and if we are attacked equally by both sides, then we must be doing something right', she recalls.

By the early 1970s, women began taking prominent positions in other walks of life. Most notably in politics. We all know how Margaret Thatcher became leader of the Conservatives in 1974 and then our first woman Prime Minister in 1979. Then during the 1980s there was what Lady Howe describes as 'quite a perceptible movement and progress'. 'Business took the attitude that it did not want its good people to go. It concentrated the mind when good people left in their mid-30s, after say a decade of training, and did not return. If you like, the bottom line cost was on the mind.'

This in turn led to more being done to encourage women to have a career and a family. At the same time work ethics were changing. Job sharing became possible. There was a movement in attitudes to part-time work.

When Lady Howe's Hansard Society Commission on Women at the Top published its findings in 1990 it had mixed news. Some had hoped that once sheer weight of numbers of women in junior management had been achieved this would, over time, generate real breakthroughs at the top. By 1995, the commission accepted that such generational change was not doing the trick, and waiting for it to do so would take far too long. Another ingredient – attitude – was needed.

In the 1980s and 1990s women had been getting to more senior positions and moved beyond 'base camp' through their own aspirations and changing attitudes. 'Women now get to the negotiating level. They are having children later.'

This coincides with a considerable boost from a change in attitude by the public at large to boardroom life. This in turn kicked legislators into life. And then from the mid-1990s there has been a raging debate on corporate governance. This matters, in the eyes of Lady Howe, because there are now new rules which enforce turnover of board positions every few years. Committees now, in theory, have a say in appointments and salary. Membership of the boardroom club is now no longer solely the gift of the chairman and companies have been forced to cast the net wider. This includes being made more aware of women.

By 1995, there were some signs of success. Around half of top company boards now contained at least one woman, whereas in 1989, 80 per cent of top companies had no women at the top. But, progress to positions of real power remained slow, with women taking influential directorships in just 3 per cent of appointments. 'Women in senior management remain hampered by glass ceilings and hemmed in by glass walls restricting their earnings and blocking them from reaching operational roles at the heart of each corporation', Lady Howe said.

During the 1990s, demographic trends helped towards women becoming a greater force at work. Speeding up of the decline in manufacturing industry in favour of the service sector helped women. In 1991, manufacturing jobs were 20 per cent of the entire workforce and by 2000 this had slipped to 17 per cent, while the business and service sector grew to a quarter of the entire workforce from 22 per cent. Also women aged 16 and upwards were becoming increasingly active in the economy. Women increasingly put back having families until their 30s and were returning to careers in greater numbers once child-birth was over.

During the last few years, Opportunity Now research shows that the number of women directors in the 200 biggest companies in Britain has doubled. But, and what a 'but' it is, this still means they hold only 6 per cent of the directorships.

Also, there has been some progress beyond the concept of a lone, token, woman. 'Having two, or more, women in the boardroom begins to look like a policy.' Second, within member organisations, one fifth of senior management positions are now occupied by women.

Lady Howe can't be sure when things will move beyond the springboard stage. It could be soon. It could be a few years, a few decades more. However, she does believe it will happen. She even reckons she will know how to judge when it has happened. Oil giant Shell appointed a woman, Liz Raynor, to its main board for the first time ever in 1998. It is part of a change in attitude by Shell as the oil company tries to raise the proportion of women in management from the present low level of 4 per cent to a more respectable 20 per cent. The appointment attracted a wave of press coverage. 'The day there is no longer comment about a woman becoming a top director is the day we have achieved success', says Lady Howe.

♀

Since its launch, the Opportunity Now campaign has grown fast. It began with a group of 61 like-minded companies and now encompasses more than 355 of the top businesses such as Sainsbury's, Glaxo-Wellcome and BP. Also many public organisations ranging from the Treasury, to the Inland Revenue, to universities and to local government.

Back in the early 1990s, women accounted for under one in ten of the managers in our businesses. Opportunity Now campaign organisations have achieved a far higher proportion of women making it to managerial level, with some 35 per cent of women reaching this status in member organisations compared with the current national average throughout the whole UK workforce of 18 per cent.

A major challenge for the campaign will be to continue to try and break the stereotypical perceptions about the kind of work women and men can do. In Britain today, women do make up nearly half of the workforce, including part-time workers. But women are concentrated at lower levels in business. They are also unevenly represented in professions. For instance, 90 per cent of nurses are women, 96 per cent of hairdressing apprentices are women, but only 20 per cent of computer analysts are women.

The macho image of engineering and construction continues to alienate women and perpetuates an unbalanced workforce.

Britain's biggest engineering and defence group BAE Systems has recognised the country has been hurt by this alienation. BAE, which recently changed its name from British Aerospace, says the UK only produces 16,000 engineers a year and is behind competitors like Japan, Germany, France and even Finland. Around 90 per cent of BAE's 115,000 staff are white males. 'This is not a healthy situation for companies like mine – at BAE Systems there is an 8 per cent growth needed in engineering recruitment', said chief executive John Weston. Against the background of a serious shortage of engineers, BAE tried to change its ways and become more attractive to women as a potential employer in 1999 and in the following year it moved from a lowly seventy-fourth in the league table of desirable employers to a more creditable twenty-third.

BAE's recruitment problem has been mirrored in other scientific and engineering companies. Industrial group Procter & Gamble said, despite having an open recruitment policy, it found that at every higher level up the executive ladder women had been falling away. It recognised it was 'wasting an enormous pool of talent' and since 1996 it became more proactive in promoting women with the result that women now make up a fifth of associate directors and above and the company says it is benefiting from a change in management culture. Also engine maker, Cummins, recognised it was perceived as a company that mainly employed men and since 1997 its drive to attract talented women has seen its number of women managers grow by 34 per cent. The result, Cummins says, is that its image as an employer has been enhanced.

Perhaps the most visible success story, in terms of women grabbing executive power, comes from Glaxo Wellcome. The drugs group was a founder member of the Opportunity Now campaign and it says 'a truly diverse workforce is essential for the wellbeing of our business and our staff'.

Over 42 per cent of the drugs manufacturer and researcher's staff are women. Glaxo recognised that having an equal opportunity profile would be seen as a key recruitment tool in a competitive business environment. So it spent £250,000 to 'pump prime' workforce diversity. A range of flexible working policies on career breaks and part-time working meant it is now possible to be promoted from secretarial grades to managerial positions, Glaxo claims. In middle management, a third of its staff are women, in senior management women now hold 16 per cent of posts and Glaxo Wellcome UK recently appointed the third woman to its board.

♀

Clara Freeman says: 'Snuffing out old-fashioned working cultures and outdated attitudes to women means companies can enjoy a huge injection of talent'.

And there seem to be benefits flowing from attracting the best workers to come through your door in the first place. One of the key aims of the campaign has been to improve business life by encouraging women to stay in the workplace. Furthermore, financial benefits will flow through from a culture of equality, says Opportunity Now.

By improving the chances of keeping the best staff, companies see real 'bottom-line' benefits. For example, Xerox UK reckons it saved £1 million in a five year period in the mid-to-late 1990s after it changed attitudes so that 80 per cent of women returned after maternity leave. Also, over the 1990s, Xerox said it doubled the number of women managers it had on its staff from 10 per cent to 20 per cent.

The problem of staff retention is even troubling the biggest accountancy and consultancy services firm – PriceWaterhouseCoopers. It recruits about 1,400 graduates each year and half of these are women. In the first eight years of the careers of these high-flyers, women maintain fifty-fifty status, but then start drifting away at a much faster rate, says head of human resources Tony Allen.

The major reason why PWC has so few women at senior level is many leave to start families and never return, partly because the work is very focused on being a slave to the client and this conflicts with satisfying the family. 'Also the white male culture of senior management is probably off-putting to many women. This is a big issue for us because it's very costly to train all our people. Losing so many female staff represents an enormous loss of skill, talent and investment', he says.

PWC sees the need to fuel growth as a major reason to make diversity of its workforce a goal. PWC needs renewal and innovation because it is competing against smaller, more agile, and more focused competitors. There is also pressure to improve the mix of the workforce from some of the 'faster moving' companies in PWC's client base, he said.

The staff retention argument is at its most potent in business sectors that have very high proportions of their staff as women, like retailing and banking.

Boots the Chemist has more than 30 per cent of its store managers as women, and further down the profile of its store sales staff as many as 94 per cent of shop supervisors are women. Obviously, in the days when only half its staff returned after maternity leave, Boots was wasting millions. So it embarked on a campaign of job sharing and flexible working to encourage its female talent to return. By eliminating lost sales performance, by saving on training costs, by saving on recruitment and uniforms and administration the stores giant reckoned it gained £1 million on to its bottom line for every 1 per cent per annum reduction in staff turnover.

Businesses covering the spectrum from banks to supermarkets also back up the commercial case. Sainsbury's has found that it costs them more than £10,000 to find, train and recruit new store managers every time a woman manager leaves and does not return.

HSBC has been seeing considerable savings since it has introduced flexible working arrangements. Indeed, as our economy becomes increasingly a '24 hour' one, the business case for flexibility strengthens. In HSBC's case this means its First Direct telephone line banking subsidiary which is open all hours of the day and night is ripe for women workers and 42 per cent of its managers are women. Meanwhile, HSBC, a founder member of Opportunity Now, has doubled its return rate from maternity leave.

In service organisations, cracking the staff retention problem also will benefit the customer because it will mean the customer will deal with more experienced staff. The Halifax, the building society that turned itself into a bank, has three-quarters of its whole staff as women. Yet, even in the late 1990s, its own staff suffered from the perception that the bank was male-dominated. Halifax reacted with its Fair's Fair initiative and recognised it needed to unlock the potential of every member of its workforce. On one level it actually wrote a commitment to equal opportunities in its business plan. The bank says 75 per cent now return after maternity leave. Also more women stayed long enough to earn senior management posts and the number of female executives rose from 7 to 19 in four years. 'Women now feel more involved and valued and staff retention has increased.'

♀

Apart from the 'bottom-line' benefits mentioned above, smart businesses also increasingly realise that they have a broader commitment to the communities and wider societies in which they operate. In this regard, there are wider business case benefits that will flow from having equality in the workforce.

Lloyds Bank, in its Female Focus 2000 research, actually put its finger on a reason why women bosses are characterised as having a 'softer' management style to their male counterparts. Female entrepreneurs are more likely to view themselves as 'creators of jobs', while male entrepreneurs said they were first and foremost 'creators of wealth'. While 43 per cent of male go-getters said growth in turnover and profits were the key markers by which they should be valued a success, only a quarter of female entrepreneurs said these were paramount. Equally, customer satisfaction was rated more highly by the women bosses. 'This shows women recognise the need to build strong foundations if they are to achieve long-term success. The fact that women see themselves as job creators highlights the growing importance of the role they play in the local community', said Lloyds.

It will be fascinating to see if women continue to play a greater and greater entrepreneurial role in the twenty-first century and whether this will in turn lead to a lasting increase in employment levels.

For now, though, there are other more immediate business benefits to be gleaned from having more women come through as bosses.

During recent decades, much has happened to make *everyone* feel less valued at work. Redundancy has struck upon a large proportion of the workforce at some time. Virtually nobody can be secure in claiming they have a 'job for life' anymore. So it is important that businesses don't just stop at recruiting and then retaining the best staff. They need to motivate them as well.

NatWest Bank found it increased motivation, and benefited financially, when it changed its ways and diversified its workforce. The bank, in a nutshell, found that the effective management and development of diverse employees increased its ability to satisfy a wider range of customers. Staff became more in tune with the needs of customers in their community. Equal opportunity policy improved business performance by raising motivation and harnessing greater potential in staff.

In industrial settings, the growth in family-friendly ways of working can be achieved at little overall cost to organisations, but these policies can pay off with significant productivity rises, Opportunity Now says.

We have already learnt how women have been an increasingly important element in the country's overall workforce and by 2001 it has even been predicted by the Institute of Employment Research they will make up half the workforce. What this tells us is that women's role as consumers will become even more powerful. Their spending power in the economy is on the up and up and in many households women already hold the purse strings.

So clever companies are having to realise that they need to be chameleons.

Leading supermarket J. Sainsbury's has a customer base that is 80 per cent female. It acknowledges the business benefit of having women in decision-making roles and during the 1990s it doubled the number of middle-managers that are women. 'They can focus on issues that men simply are not aware of', said Sainsbury.

In organisations where the workforce is in direct contact with the customer, like retailers, education, health providers and in financial services, there is a business advantage in a workforce profile which reflects the customer profile, says Opportunity Now. The 'bottom-line' benefits come from making your customers feel more comfortable and this in turn makes it less likely they will defect to a rival. Also businesses can benefit from feedback from the workforce into business strategy and product development. For companies which have 'ethical' motives as part of their mission in life, like Glaxo Wellcome and its research into drugs that will save and enhance life, having a good equal opportunities image is essential as a starting point to gaining credibility in its ethical claims. Lastly, a high affinity with the customer base in itself boosts the corporate reputation and image and this in turn is reflected in customer loyalty and sales.

♀

Opportunity Now member organisations are different from the rest in that they have been more successful in promoting talented women to the top of the tree. This shows through with 8 per cent of executive directors within member organisations being women. A further 23 per cent of non-executive directors and subsidiary board directors are women, a far brighter picture than seen across the business world in general.

Furthermore, in government departments that belong to the campaign and in public appointments to the list of the 'great and good' to serve on public boards, women are getting the nod like never before.

What sets apart Opportunity Now members from their counterparts is a much more formal and demonstrable commitment to equal opportunities. About 75 per cent of members have someone at main board level with responsibility for gender issues. Similarly, 73 per cent of members have formal policies in place to support goals for equality for women. The Opportunity Now organisations, as one might expect are more proactive on gaining feedback on gender issues and policies. Tribunal cases should be well publicised and not 'covered up' so the costs in monetary terms and image terms of discrimination should be understood throughout the workforce, it says. Also they are typically much more enthusiastic backers for flexible working time practices and more enthusiastic in complying with parental leave legislation.

The latest research from the campaign and its Catalyst partner in the USA suggests that chief executives are waking up to the business case for promoting women to the top. First, 65 per cent of CEOs recognise that 'women have a significant consumer base whose power is growing'. More cold-heartedly, 56 per cent say the likelihood of anti-discrimination lawsuits is growing. Forty-two per cent say shareholders are demanding more women at senior levels. Therefore, self-preservation dictates CEOs do something.

The Opportunity Now campaign has the support of 37 of the country's biggest corporations in the FTSE 100 index. In the campaign's early days it did not score well in attracting the big investment banks and City institutions to sign up to its views. This was disappointing given the evidence of sexual harassment and prejudice that prevented women rising to the top in this world that has been written about elsewhere. 'An area particularly known for the challenges it presents to women's progression and entry to traditionally male roles', says Opportunity Now. Currently, nine City firms have joined the campaign. But clearly there is a long way to go.

Top board level positions 'remain heavily male dominated'. Also, the campaign admits it has not yet done enough to make the business case for working on gender issues.

A specific target, according to Opportunity Now leader Clara Freeman, is to expand the campaign by making sure its membership tops the 500 mark. Also, she wants to try to double the number of members from the top 200 companies in the country.

The Prime Minister, Tony Blair, has backed the campaign. 'It is essential to the economic future of our country that everyone, regardless of gender, has the opportunity to achieve their full potential at work. It is vital to encourage a society that supports and values the contribution of all its citizens. I believe the activities of Opportunity Now show the way forward in tackling the economic and career disadvantages which women still face', he said.

The challenge the campaign sets itself for early in the twenty-first century is to have made a measurable improvement to the quality and extent of women's employment at all levels.

# 10

# *Squaring the Circle*

## 'Clubbing With The Men'

For decades men have been setting the rules in the business world. This means rules surrounding the room at the top – the boardroom. But, equally importantly, also setting the agenda for the paths that lead to the boardroom. Membership of the plush London clubs and sporting havens has been like a 'base camp' for men *en route* to the pinnacle of the largest companies.

With success in the latest campaign to allow women to belong to the most famous and influential sporting club in the world – the MCC – there are signs that things are changing.

Women had been banned from membership of the home of cricket, Marylebone Cricket Club, for some 211 years. Then in 1999, after an initial failure to overturn the rules in 1991, a second ballot of the 17,500-strong membership won the right for women to be allowed to join for the first time. Rachael Heyhoe Flint, former England Captain, one of the most famous sportswomen ever and now a businesswoman, was influential in winning change at the MCC. She was one of the first women members elected and we shall cover her story later.

However, top clubs in London do still resist moves to offer equal membership rights to women. The gentlemen-only Savile Club was the latest to turn down a change in rules.

Best-known is The Garrick Club, a club named after a famous actor turned theatre entrepreneur and situated in West-End theatreland. Its walls are adorned by an amazing array of pictures of hundreds of the most famous actors and actresses. Ornate dining rooms, bars and private rooms help explain why the club's popularity extends way beyond the artistic world to very senior politicians, top civil servants, lawyers, judges, publishers and editors. In a quaint joke, that is typical of the English 'establishment', openly using the Garrick for 'business' is not allowed. But members of The Garrick don't pay thousands a year to belong just to feed themselves in very agreeable surroundings. They acknowledge the attraction of 'belonging' means dining with and drinking with contacts that are used to gain influence, information and business leads in a way not possible elsewhere. In this way, The Garrick is a very exclusive club and a club that women can't belong to. It has survived attempts to drop the chauvinist barriers. But in truth, it had a £50 million inheritance from the estate of famous author of *Winnie the Pooh*, A. A. Milne, and has no need to alter its ways to survive financially.

A victory in breaking down the barriers at the MCC, the so-called 'Male Chauvinist Club', will have an impact beyond the ground that has a few of the most hallowed acres in Britain. But this impact could be small compared to the impact made as women build up clubs and networks of their own.

Women have tried to grow bolt holes of their own. In the late 1990s, architect Susan Harrison came close to opening her own Bloomsbury Club, born out of her experience of changing work patterns and aimed at 'movers and shakers', but she was frustrated on three possible properties. 'I had to balance all the plates on all the sticks and found that any one of them might not land and trip you up.'

However, the Parrot Club, based in the Basil Street hotel at the back of Harrods, used to have a fuddy-duddy image but now says it attracts 'a number of younger members who have set up their own businesses and need somewhere to entertain clients'. And the London Ladies' Club, with a wider cultural and social networking outlook, has 'Opening doors across the capital' as its motto.

♀

HighTech Women is a networking club that is going places, and fast. Founded by Lucy Marcus in spring 2000, it has already grown to include more than 1500 of the country's young, bright, women entrepreneurs.

HighTech Women meet in the University Women's Club, housed in a stylish, old-worldy pile in Audley Square in one of the poshest parts of London in Mayfair close to the Dorchester and Hyde Park. The UWC was founded in 1886, but the links with previous centuries and the HighTech Women end right there.

Lucy Marcus runs her own venture capital and consultancy firm, Marcus Venture Consulting, which she started in April 1999. The manner in which HTW was born shows how fast things can change for ambitious women in this high-tech age. Lucy said she remembers attending a high-profile conference on new economy business run by Atlas Consulting. 'I was one of four women there out of more than 200. I met all the other three women in the closet! That made me think: "it is time we got out of the closet". So I set out on the idea of a club for meeting and mentoring', Lucy said.

First, she set up HTW by word-of-mouth recommendations of her acquaintances in the tech economy. The HTW does not charge membership fees and is funded by sponsors from the big corporations. Also Lucy was determined it should be 'self-defining' in that anyone who wanted to join, could do so. 'It is not just about people who have made it. We are about reaching out.'

In tune with the times, HTW launched itself with a website presence. Lucy was amazed to find that, within the first three days, the site had attracted 1,000 'hits' from interested women in the UK and around the world.

In keeping with the self-defining qualifications needed to belong to HTW, its membership is a broad sweep of any woman who has connections with the new economy. It stretches from MBA students, making up about 10 per cent, to chief executives and essentially self-made entrepreneurs of new dot coms forming another 10 per cent of members at the top of the scale. The 80 per cent in between are a whole array of, mostly young, chief technology officers, headhunters, PR professionals, telecoms/communications workers, web designers and those from other professions thrust into contact with technology due to their work.

Louise Tingstrom, who was head of PR and marketing for Ant Factory, one of the largest so-called incubators that fund the Internet start-ups, is a member because she believes in the 'responsibility to mentor and to share the passion of our business'. Sue Blackman, a partner with Deloittes, says the club gave her the confidence to go for the job she felt she was capable of. Penny Jerram, MD of Defining Edge, her own retail services business, says: 'HTW is incredibly useful. Anything that gives you an angle that means people are willing to be more receptive is valuable.'

Lucy Marcus is confident enough to predict: 'In the next five years, we will see emerge from HTW the equivalent of the next Marjorie Scardino'.

The HTW meet a couple of times a month. One area of activity is large, open, gatherings with a theme or industry, like marketing. Members will gather for early evening drinks and a conversation in the University Women's Club library, a room about the same size and ambience of a country house drawing room. When they get round to the meeting proper, the atmosphere is still jovial. Lucy will go round the room and make everyone introduce themselves. The members seem confident individuals and in the majority of cases are not shy about talking about successes, or hurdles they have hit. Very much a live-wire, Lucy also has an amazing capacity to make connections. 'You should speak to so and so, and her, and then her', she will tell her audience while, in the next breath, posing a searching question about just how the member's business is going. The other area is more specialist gatherings for say, finance directors.

An ongoing element of the HTW is providing a 'directors pool', a kind of database that can be dipped into whenever the network hears about a company needing to find top executive talent. Capable mentors, advisers and non-executive directors are fundamental to the success of any business, be it a start-up or a mature public company.

Building a strong diverse board of directors with experienced and knowledgeable non-executive directors is key to the success of any company. By the same token, creating such a board can be very challenging. To that end HighTech Women has created its own pool.

At one recent gathering of HighTech Women, a senior director of the leading venture capital firm 3i, formerly known as Investors in Industry, passed on tips about how boards should work in the future. In the past boardrooms have been guided by the narrow aims of 'finding a right strategy, the right resources and keeping out of jail'. Non-executive directors have too often been mere 'Teddy Bears', 'who can be thrown in the corner and not answer back'. The venture capital director said we must learn to change board personnel frequently enough to fit in with changing situations. For aspiring women his tip was: 'Leave a clear impression of what you are good at and a clear impression of what you want to achieve'.

'It is very hard for women in general to get that all-important first directorship role', Lucy Marcus says. 'In thinking about what makes HighTech Women unusual in the field of women's groups, I think it is the foundation upon which it is built – one of meeting and mentoring. It is a completely open group, with no "screening procedure" so anyone who finds it of interest can come and join in, and it is a supportive and friendly group that applauds the accomplishments of its members. The fact that students are valued and thought of as equals, with experiences and contributions to make of their own, is integral to helping to build their self-confidence so that they can go on to become business leaders themselves. The networks that people are able to create via HighTech Women are the key to the success for businesses and businesswomen across the board', the founder believes.

Lucy, who herself went to Harvard, worked for the US Treasury's economic policy side and then did a postgraduate degree at Cambridge, is typical of women making waves quickly in the new technology revolution. She was responsible for Marketing and Business Development for Europe, the Middle East and Africa at Infinity Financial Technologies, and worked at Price Waterhouse in the East European Services Division.

Listed as a 'face to watch' in *Management Today* magazine's annual list of Britain's 50 Most Powerful Women, Lucy is a non-executive director of a number of companies and sits on the University of Cambridge Judge Institute of Management Advisory Board, and is a member of the Wellesley College Business Leadership Council. She says her HighTech Women networking club is: 'All about meeting and mentoring and recognising that we each have our own special skills'.

Lucy sees the funny side of the image of Americans being obsessed with the Royal family. She will openly tell all and sundry that her real ambition is 'to E the Queen'. Referring to the fact that it is not yet possible to send a personal e-mail to her majesty, Lucy says 'I want to be the first to put a new 'e' in Queen!'

'I have always been a Wild West type of person. When I started, there was really only established venture capitalists like Investors in Industry around', she said. Her Marcus Ventures gets in '300 business plans a month' from hopefuls wanting funding to get them on their way. In 1999, she said that only about 1 per cent of these new plans would be coming in from women. Now, no doubt helped by her lead at HTW, about 15 per cent of the proposals are from women.

Lucy is attracted to working in the UK, rather than her native America, because 'the UK is an exciting place to have knowledge'. Her big tip is: 'Suck the marrow out of every opportunity that comes along, because it may not come along again'.

♀

Helena Dennison is a business woman in her own right and leads the City Women's Network. She has seen the 'networking business' grow in leaps and bounds since its cottage industry days of the 1970s. Women in Management started in 1969, but has been criticised for using 'loose' membership criteria that include, for instance, top personal assistants. Since the 1980s, whole new specialist networks have been spawned, for example, Women in Publishing, Banking, Journalism and even Computing.

Just how and why women's networks have taken off reflects in a fascinating way how the business world is changing. The Women's Institutes were born in 1915 but had to wait until summer 2000 until they had their most influential hour, as Prime Minister Tony Blair found to his cost with the backlash to his poorly-received political speech to the WI.

Helena's City Women's Network began in 1978. 'At that time, the City was filled by men in dark suits and the only women you saw were secretaries. Now we see women in the City at every single level. I like to think the CWN helped pioneer women being accepted in a responsible way', she says.

At the outset, CWN was made up totally of what Helena describes as '100 per cent big, corporation women'. These were women who worked for City-based lawyers, bankers and accountants and by and large they were professional women who did not have families. The CWN would meet, in secret, at lunchtimes in Fan Makers' Hall, a typical City livery hall venue.

Then during the late 1980s, City rents took off to astronomical levels. This forced many financial and City-based businesses to move away from the Square Mile. At the same time as a greater geographical spread emerged, the membership of the CWN diversified and it now has 43 per cent of its ranks as 'entrepreneurial women running their own businesses'. The harshening of culture in City life, Helena explains, means today 'it is simply not acceptable for women, or anyone, to take three-hour lunches'. So this means the CWN now more often meets in the evenings and away from City venues at places like the London Theatres or even out on the social season circuit at places like Glyndebourne.

The CWN costs £100 a year to join and it says events 'are not stuffy'. Members like to let their hair down and like to meet in an all-woman setting where 'having to worry about appealing to someone of the opposite sex is taken out of the equation'. However, the 160-odd CWN is 'quite elitist' in its attitude to who can belong, says Helena.

She herself was forced to make money for herself when she was widowed, with children, at the age of 29. 'I still see people bringing up young girls and giving them the assumption that they will find men who will always look after them. This is worrying', says the CWN Chair.

Helena started as a fashion designer and she says she designed some of the first skin-tight aerobics gear and coloured wet suits to be seen in the UK. Later she moved to the US telephone group GTE and as head of tele-marketing introduced a rival directory to the Yellow Pages in the UK. 'It was after being made redundant that friends told me not to work for anyone else again and work for myself', says Helena. Today, she has her own consultancy advising on communication skills and behavioural change.

♀

'I spent a lot of time waiting for people to come and find me. Only in the last few years have women used networking in the way that men have for decades', Helena says about the reason why CWN is needed.

In the early days, women were attracted to networks because they needed to counter the feelings of loneliness and isolation. To take just one example, in the law, at about the time England won the World Cup in 1966, there were approximately 600 women solicitors in the whole country, about 5 per cent of the profession at the time.

Isolation is a feeling your author can now empathise with. Being invited as a fly-on-the-wall guest at a HighTech Women gathering of about 70, made up entirely of the opposite sex, I felt like a sheepish figure out of place. I could only agree when an HTW member pleasantly said to me: 'Now you know what it feels like to be on your own in a room full of a peer-group totally of men!'

The long hours culture prevalent in business also induces stress. This complaint is shared by women and men alike and the emergence of women's networks opens up a release from stress by offering a place to talk. Networking clubs also provide an opportunity to share the problems of trying to find a work-life balance.

Networks probably evolved with the prime aim of tackling these 'human' problems associated with top women lacking the necessary 'critical mass'. But, as we shall see, women's networks are now moving into more 'kick ass' mode. They are aiming to influence.

Strange as it may seem, in an age when popular culture seems to be dominated by 'girl power' from the Spice Girls to the It Girls, the CWN thinks its top women find they are less visible than men. 'People in very senior positions do not get there by being anonymous. Increasingly, women are finding it necessary to be seen inside their businesses. It is not sufficient to be capable, to achieve. It is essential for working women to make achievements clear to others who matter', says Helena. Networks provide a sympathetic environment to try and build accurate self-promotion skills.

'To succeed, women have to commit themselves to taking full command of their reputations and destinies and accept full responsibility for how they profile and manage their careers', Helena said.

Another thing holding back women is a lack of confidence, says the CWN. This is being eroded as generations of women become more qualified.

But, the 'Old Boys' Network' still exerts a fundamental hold. As men become more senior there is a collusion at the highest levels not to challenge competence. There is a 'closed circle of contacts' at the top level of business which men have built for themselves over years and years of 'clubbing'. For men, who are in roles senior enough already to make themselves available to step up to the very top layer, there seems sufficient assumption they will be fit to perform effectively as the absolute boss. At the absurd level, this means graduates, male or female, and juniors joining from another company, can be subjected to endless rounds of tests and interviews whereas a chief executive might get the job because he knows the chairman!

The CWN members also value the coaching they get in skills to help them gain power.

♀

'Until women reach the top roles in companies, where they affect decision-making and control finances, they will not be able to fundamentally change organisations. To do this they need to increase self-confidence, become visible, accept they cannot be always liked, learn to take calculated risks and demand recognition', says Dennison.

Also, if women want to break the final glass ceilings, they need to 're-focus their efforts, examine their behaviour and do the personal soul-searching necessary to demand different ways of doing business', she believes. Stereotyping from the past portrayed women in terms of being nurturing, selfless, yielding, gentle and a batch of other 'feminine' attributes. Male managers from central casting would be presumed to be aggressive, dominant, self-reliant, ambitious etc.

However, since the late 1980s there has been a re-evaluation of businesses' role in the community and a re-evaluation in the way they should behave. Successful companies in the new century will be those that are decentralised, people-orientated, flatter structured and built on team principles, says the CWN Chair.

Will this mean bosses will survive less well on typical male traits and perform better with more appropriate female traits? The answer, when it comes, will be fascinating. In the meantime, networking will help women cope with ingrained perceptions about management.

♀

We have seen how networks are helping women to advance themselves. These networks written about so far, help women by giving them more confidence and by helping those women near the top to feed off each other for inspiration.

The networks also vary in how exclusive they are and in the way they go about things. Forum UK can be put in a different networking league. It is openly exclusive. And as such it is interesting because its members have already 'made it'. It is a network that is out to achieve real power and influence.

Dame Barbara Mills QC is a leading light in the network and has been one of the most powerful women in the country.

She stood out in a legal career of her own which saw her become the first woman to be the top criminal lawyer in the country when she was Director of Public Prosecutions for six years. This role meant she headed the Crown Prosecution Service and a staff of 6,000.

When she was appointed in 1992, she also was something of a ground-breaker because her rank also carried the status of a Permanent Secretary. She was one of the first women to fly so high in the civil service and only one of a handful ever to be made head of a government department.

Barbara Mills used her recent leadership of Forum UK since 1998 to make the organisation much more proactive. Under her, a 'very important pool' of top women is brought to the attention of the government and ministers are encouraged to dip into this pool to select women for top appointments.

The Forum is made up of a couple of hundred women of distinction. It is deliberately not open to everyone and its members pay £250 to join and £215 a year for the privilege. 'We have got there. We are happy and generally well off. We don't need our profiles splurged across the papers. In fact, most of us are sick of publicity', Barbara Mills says. The Forum 'turns the tables on the gents. It was formed when we women discovered that other networks were not open', says former leader Geraldine Sharpe-Newton, who gained prominence in the media business. Its purpose is to bring together women at the most senior level in their professions. This means trying to encourage opportunities in roles of major influence, both at the top in business and culturally, she explained.

Barbara, who was a scholar at Oxford and subsequently made a Fellow of her college, Lady Margaret Hall, remembers being repulsed by the way networks and clubs barred women in the past. For instance, she resented 'being treated like a second class citizen by the Oxford and Cambridge Club'.

Perhaps, because of this, she was determined Forum would go about gaining influence 'through the front doors' and not by the back door methods often used by male networkers in the past. 'We are not an old boy network. We are a "New Girl" network. I am adamant we should not go via the back door. This means proper procedures – the front door', said the top lawyer.

Barbara was called to the bar as a barrister in 1963, got noticed as a senior prosecutor on behalf of the Inland Revenue and was made a Queen's Counsel in 1986. For two years in the 1990s she was Director of the Serious Fraud Office and since stepping down as DPP in 1998 she has held the new position of The Adjudicator, a kind of ombudsman fighting maladministration cases at the Inland Revenue and Customs and Excise. When she began on her career, Barbara says there definitely was an anti-woman prejudice and 'you tended not to get an easy life'. She rose to the top and managed a family, even though she says 'I was very lucky that my career really took off when my youngest of four kids was already 16'.

The job of being the top prosecutor in the country was one 'I wouldn't have missed for the world', she said. However, 'life was very unforgiving'. Barbara Mills says being DPP was the ultimate 24-hour, seven day a week job. 'I was on call the whole time. It got wearing having to tell

staff where you are going to be every minute of every day.
. . . It is quite a lonely sensation at the top. The Forum
helps provide connections that a middle-class, white and
successful man has had naturally', she says.

The network, via its worldwide parent, the International
Women's Forum, has its roots stretching back nearly 30
years to the time when Elinor Guggenheimer set up her
network in New York in 1970. Jean Denton, who later
became Baroness Denton after a political career and
serving as a DTI minister, was the Forum's first UK head.
'Forum is an organisation for women of distinction. We
want to make society better by being active in it.' There
you have it. Club together on the basis of a real desire for
change.

Then delve deeper into what membership of this
network offers and you see how the benefits flow. Every
month the club has a breakfast meeting at The Ritz hotel.
Barbara Mills says these are the most popular events among
Forum members. Each month, on a mid-week day between
about 7.45 a.m. and 9 a.m. forty or fifty top women will
try and put the world to rights over coffee, croissants and
fine silverware at The Ritz.

Here, apart from whatever the formal agenda might be,
these power breakfasters 'share the pain and exhilaration
of personal stories. This helps make up for lack of support
from the men. It can be inspirational and supportive. I go
back to my office totally energised', says Geraldine Sharpe-
Newton.

Several times a year the Forum has power lunches as
well. Recent special guests have ranged from Margaret Jay
and the writer Beryl Bainbridge. 'We get access to places
where others can't get access to', claims the present leader.
Forum's membership is very London-based and this special
access saw them don hard hats and visit the Tate Modern
gallery before it opened to the public. Also, Forum organ-
ises a series of 'Dinearounds' which see a cluster of eight
or ten gather for the evening in the house of a member.

'It is high level conversation, we do not go in for "girly" chat', says Barbara Mills.

This again shows how the Forum can be set apart from other networks which, in atmosphere, would reflect more hair being let down. Forum UK defines eligibility for membership as 'top women'. 'This ranges from justice and law, Parliamentarians, corporate executives of major companies including Chairs and Presidents and Chief Executives, to well established entrepreneurs of accomplishment, renowned artists, humanitarians and journalists whose work is known and respected far beyond the communities in which they work and live, and also those renowned in the voluntary sector', says Forum's secretary Liz Harman. In spring 2001, Celia Goodhart became Forum's leader. She is at the top of the education profession as Principal of the Queen's College girls' school.

A prospective candidate should have demonstrated leadership within her field and within her community. A candidate should clearly be a powerful person and a woman directly responsible for policy making decisions within her organisation. Those wishing to join the network should also have:

- demonstrated interest and involvement beyond her chosen field
- an ability, interest and time to be active in a national/ international network
- leadership in a field not already over-represented in Forum UK
- a willingness to be an active member and fulfil any financial requirements of membership. She should currently be involved actively in her profession or field of endeavour.

For Geraldine Sharpe-Newton, the ideas of Gloria Steinem and her concept of the 'Girl Gang' have been an inspiration. Forum UK's guiding principle in self-help takes a cue from Gloria's belief that women 'must always put a hand out to take another along'. Specifically in corporate life, this should mean a lone woman with power on a company board must fill a boardroom chair with another one. 'Mentoring is the major issue. This means looking after younger women on the way up. Teaching them how to prepare for boards. How to achieve full potential', says Geraldine.

Geraldine's credentials as an eminent woman in business are impressive, having reached the top in the media world on both sides of the Atlantic. She can lay claim to launching *The Economist* magazine in the USA in 1978 while working at agency Burson-Marsteller. She worked her way up the public relations tree to become head of communications for Cable News Network International in 1995. In this job she was PR chief for Europe, the Middle East and Africa at Ted Turner's media and entertainments empire before setting up her own consultancy in 1998.

Asked about the impact of her Forum, Geraldine sees it has done 'measurable good for the place of women in leadership'. Also she acknowledges the emotional element to self-help. At its most basic level the Forum is 'a safe place for women to turn to for advice'. On another level, it is valuable for 'knowledge building and sharing of ideas'.

This outlet of self-help is undoubtedly valuable. But something more is needed for real dividends of change. 'Women must be in a position to impact on the bottom line. To hold the key positions. Otherwise you can reach the top of your profession, but not the top of the company.' The different success rates for men and women in reaching the top cannot adequately be explained by different personalities, in her view. 'Women can be as tough and difficult as any man. Men can also be soft and cuddly. Women may usually be better at gathering consensus.'

Membership of Forum UK has brought tangible rewards for businesswoman Peggy Dannenbaum. She became the first ever woman to sit on the board of chocolates maker Thorntons plc after being headhunted by another member of the club. Also Peggy was made Vice Chair of a huge NHS board covering the London boroughs of Barnet and Edgware by the former Tory Health Secretary, Virginia Bottomley, as a result of connections with former Minister for Small Business and Forum member, Baroness Jean Denton. 'If people are looking for qualified women, the Forum is the place to go', Peggy says.

The Forum network may have the essence of what is required in that it stresses the training aspect of self-help: the nuts and bolts that are needed to put women in place to join the candidates list for a directorship. There is the major international annual conference and regular news letters. Forum is elitist. With networks in 16 countries worldwide, the largest groups are in the USA and the UK. Membership is deliberately nurtured to run to around 200 or so in the UK. 'To be seen as a talent pool. Small enough so people say "if you're a member, you have arrived".'

As to results, Geraldine Sharpe-Newton jokes, men 'could be rattled . . . they want to know what we are up to'. Where women have made it to the top table they have made it a more attractive and interesting place, she thinks. 'We bring a fresh approach. The component of diversity is a very healthy thing, but I don't want tokenism.'

Will the networks spark a revolution in the boardroom? 'Marks and Spencer did not have a woman on board for decades, though it has always been a superb company and served its customers well. In the short term, I am more likely to go to the moon than see 50 women running public companies. But, to quote Stella Rimington, former woman boss of MI5, 'we will give people road maps for the future . . . to do things that have not been done before'.

♀

During 1999–2000, the first women honorary members won their places at the MCC.

Cynics said the MCC was forced to change its ways because, unlike the super-rich Garrick Club, it needed to drag itself into the modern age on commercial grounds alone. The club's previous all-male membership stance had meant that two major sponsors had withdrawn offers of support, unhappy at the sexist status. More importantly, a £4.5 million application for a National Lottery grant to help rebuild Lords was turned down because the MCC's membership rule fell foul of sex discrimination rules.

Rachael Heyhoe Flint symbolised the absurd nature of the old MCC regime. For she, simply, is one of the best cricketers and sports personalities this country has ever produced. As such, she deserved to be able to mingle with lesser men in the Lords Pavilion.

Rachael captained the England team for 11 years and made a record number of appearances in a 23-year career from 1960 to 1983. She made history by leading the first ever women's team to play at Lords when she captained England versus Australia in 1976. As a player she holds the record for the largest score by an English player in women's test matches in England with her innings of 179. After retiring at international level, she was Chairman of the Women's Cricket Association for two years. She has four books to her name. Also she played hockey for England and played for her county for 25 years and also played squash and golf for Staffordshire.

Alongside her career as a sporting star, Rachael established herself as a journalist and media figure. 'I kind of talked my way into becoming a sports journalist', she said and within four years of joining her local paper, the *Wolverhampton Chronicle*, in 1965 she had been made sports editor. She later became Britain's first woman sports presenter with a job at ITV on the *World of Sport*, wrote for the *Daily* and *Sunday Telegraph* and in 1973 even was named as Best After Dinner Speaker by the guild of professional toastmasters.

Since, Rachael has said she has never had to ask for a job in her life and she is a perfect example of those who have used sport as a passport into business. 'People got to know my name', Rachael remembers.

She was made a director of Family Assurance Friendly Society on the back of the chairman hearing her make a speech. When, in 1977, she lost the England captaincy, despite having the highest batting average of all the players at the time, the chairman of Wolverhampton Wanderers FC 'was so outraged' he made her a director. She is currently in charge of community public relations for the club and also is in business on her own as a promotions and marketing consultant for the Hyatt La Manga club resort and the Patshull Park country club.

The star sportswoman sparked the move for change at the MCC in 1991 after her own application for membership was turned down. 'I always like a challenge in life. But I didn't do it for feminist reasons, I only pushed for women to be members because I thought it was best for cricket in general', she said.

What motivated Rachael to pursue her application for eight years until she was rewarded with honorary membership in 1999? 'I didn't want any favours, or any queue-jumping. It was just about ladies being considered as human beings', she says.

Furthermore, Rachael realised to change MCC, a private club, even though it is such an influential institution, it would not have worked to 'go rampaging up and down St John's Road outside the MCC – because that would have turned even more men against us'. Instead she needed to win the argument on intellectual grounds. The MCC rules needed a 66 per cent majority of its 18,000 members to vote in favour for them to be changed. These thousands of male members had themselves had to go through an average 16 year waiting list to join. So, it was going to take something special to shake them up.

Rachael had influential people on her side. Famous mus-
ical producer Sir Tim Rice and the late, great, commentator
Brian Johnston, were her prime backers. Also the then club
President Colin Ingleby-Mackenzie, who, when the vote
was won in 1999 said: 'I am delighted and excited by the
decision. Women are a very fine species.' Rachael said the
decision to award honorary membership to women was:
'Wonderful news, but it has been a rather long gestation
period from when I first applied. This means as much to
me today as the honour of captaining my country.'

There are lessons to be learned from Rachael's story. In
the historic ballot, 4,072 men voted against, but 9,394 men
were convinced in her favour. She could not have won the
day without changing the opinions of thousands of men
and without getting famous men 'onside'. Indeed, it is a
theme that Helena Dennison, the head of the City Women's
Network we learnt about earlier, picks up on. She raises
the prospect of women and men networking in each
other's company as a way forward. 'Women still perceive
a need to network with other women, but if they are to
make their mark in business as people and on the basis of
competence, then I believe we should explore the question of whether their networking should also include men',
she says.

Asked about the impact of allowing women to join the
MCC, Rachael Heyhoe Flint says: 'The actual atmosphere
in the Pavilion at Lords hasn't changed in the slightest. We
are, after all, only a dozen women in a pavilion that holds
betweeen 2,000 and 3,000. However, the MCC has begun
to field a women's team on the pitch, made up of associate
women members. It will be a very slow process, but in two
or three decades there could be more equal numbers of
women with the men sitting in the Long Room.'

We will have to see if this will influence a move to them
filling the important seats in the boardrooms of our
companies.

# 11

## *Tales of the City*

♀

Women, in increasing numbers, have been coming through as entrepreneurs and become darlings in the eyes of the City. This means they have been at the very top of companies that have grown fast and been quoted on the stockmarket. While this brings paper fortunes, there has been the glare of public scrutiny and attention as well. It is fascinating to observe how women entrepreneurs have coped. Also how some have risen to control the purse-strings as finance directors of large publicly-quoted groups. And, for the purposes of this book, it is fascinating to look at how some women have shot to fame, but then faded from public view.

♀

Kate Bleasdale can claim to be one of the people who has made the most out of a nursing career. After graduate training and a successful career of her own in nursing, she first made a fortune with her novel idea for staff management systems for hospitals.

That was in her mid-20s. A dozen years later, Kate Bleasdale led the company that spearheaded the idea of private, walk-in and pay, doctor services in Britain.

Nowadays, the main arm of her business – running a handful of medical staff agency chains – is going 'full pelt'.

Kate's story is fascinating. She has experienced the real extremes of 'making it in the City' and then falling out of favour fast.

As a young, female 'go-getter' she stood out. For her role as chief executive of the public company that launched 'Medicentres' she was feted as 'Entrepreneur of the Year' in 1997. In the good stockmarket times she was worth several millions on paper. Conceivably, had her business taken off as she hoped and shaken up the established National Health Service near-monopoly in the UK, she might have been Britain's first woman chief executive of a large FTSE company. But, as we shall see, she became sick of the City. Her plc was taken off the market in 1999. Today, in private hands, it has annual turnover of more than £125 million and if it thrives we can only wonder at what might have been. Kate has grown a company that now has 600 staff and approaching 90,000 registered on its agencies' books, while running a family of four boys. And she believes that as a businesswomen she should be treated no different than a man.

The essences of Kate Bleasdale's success are her instincts and professional nursing training which enabled her to come up with innovative ideas to cure inefficiencies in the health service. The other elements are, having courage of her convictions and the guts to go out and do things.

It is interesting to look over distinct phases in Kate's career that formed her path to the top.

♀

She started out by graduating from the Chelsea College of Nursing in 1983. From there she completed a masters degree at Kings Hospital in London and went on to work at Putney Hospital. By the age of 25 she had been promoted to be a sister in charge of a staff of 120. Pretty impressive. But even at this stage Kate was realising her personality, and ambition, meant she was unlikely to stay within the NHS. 'I have always been a bit of a maverick. I didn't think I was cut out to bide my time and work my way up the ladder, so I began to look for an opportunity to be my own boss.'

She felt all her time was taken up organising staffing rotas. A specific spur was when she turned up for duty at 7 a.m. one Saturday to find there were not enough nurses and she had to trawl through 10 agencies and pull in inexperienced staff. Kate had to work two and half shifts herself and left thinking 'there must be a better way'.

She set out with colleague John Cariss, who is now her husband, to build a register of good nurses and set up a computer system. They borrowed £20,000 and remortgaged the house and eventually got the first big break when St Heliers Hospital, Carshalton, took on their idea. As the business got off the ground with a staff of just four, Kate remembers 'being on call all day and every day for three years'.

♀

The company and its product really started to go forward when Kate Bleasdale, on the advice of a former professor, put in for and won a national nursing award.

However, it was hard graft with modest reward at first. Kate was starting her family at this time and is quick to acknowledge 'the wonderful support' of her nanny who has stayed with her for eight years now and who was, in the early days, taking home more than the boss. 'I was working from a tiny office. For the first three years, I couldn't afford to take more than £800 a month out of the business for myself, although my partner was still employed by the hospital. The nanny was getting paid £850 a month. I didn't have any money for myself at all and I managed to run up a nice little overdraft.'

So how did she cope? 'You just do things. There was no one else to run the agency. You just get used to it. My motivation was I could see a gap in the market, no one else was doing it. What we were doing was very innovative and that drives you on to do things.'

By 1990 the company had 30,000 nurses on its books and had won seven staff management system contracts with hospitals.

♀

At this stage, around four to five years after the business was set up, Kate was able to pay herself 'a living wage'.

The business of staff management, that began with an investment of £20,000, was now on a course that would lead to being a publicly-quoted company worth tens of millions.

By 1995, the annual turnover had grown to £2.2 million and Bleasdale was ready to extend her ambitions. This took shape in a merger with another medical company which was an agency business placing General Practitioner doctors run by Michael Sinclair.

This is the decision which Kate Bleasdale describes as being the most difficult in her comparatively short business career to date. Seeing control and total ownership of the business they founded, lost, was the most difficult thing for her and her partner.

'I wasn't really planning to run a public company. And I do not see myself as someone who carefully plans out my career years in advance. It almost happened by accident. The drive for me has been to be in place as the best person to grow the group', Kate says.

The faint-hearted could not even contemplate taking on the extra responsibility and extra personal demands, at a time when babies were arriving at regular, two-year intervals in the Bleasdale household.

Kate earns a salary of around £180,000 as chief executive. And the shares in Sinclair Montrose Healthcare, the company she grew from nothing, were worth more than £2 million.

'I'm sure I'm the highest paid qualified nurse in the country, not much doubt about that', she says, not gloating, but taking satisfaction that the incredible hard work and long hours have been rewarded.

But it now seems it was another natural stepping stone. In the early years, all profits had been reinvested in the business to keep up with new technology. Kate says there were offers from trade buyers for the company, but these were turned down because she felt they undervalued a business in its 'immature stage'. By 1996 the need to fund the continuing growth of the business, which now had over 40 hospital staffing contracts, saw Sinclair Montrose Healthcare join the stockmarket. In 1997 the group had annual sales of £20 million and a second share issue raised more funds to fuel the next big project – Medicentres.

♀

Perhaps because Kate herself was part of a family of eight children, she privately admits she would have liked two more. A hankering not shared by her partner. Well, introducing Medicentres in Britain can be likened to having another couple of babies in terms of the impact on Kate's life.

Medicentres provide medical care for 'walk-in' patients who are prepared to pay for their treatment. In other words, people who can afford at least the £40 basic consultation fee and who value seeing a doctor when they want to and not being subject to the frustrations of NHS home-town doctors.

The idea was launched in Britain with the first Medi-centre at Victoria Station. Another eight were introduced between 1996 and 1998 and in December 1998 a new batch of openings took the chain up to a dozen.

Sinclair Montrose and existing private health insurers, like BUPA, say research shows potentially between 25 per cent and 30 per cent of the population would pay for treatment. 'If the potential of private care materialises across the country then logically the UK would have 2,000 Medicentres.'

'We are on the verge of creating something that is part of very big changes in the way healthcare is provided in the UK', said Kate Bleasdale.

And heading Sinclair Montrose at a time of rapid expan-sion and under the public gaze has been 'The steepest learning curve of my life', says Kate about the time on the stockmarket. Not only had a dozen of the Medicentres been born in the first two years, there were ambitious plans to double this number during 1999 in partnership with stores like Boots and Sainsbury's. But in addition, Sinclair Mont-rose has been making acquisitions to the medical staff agencies arm.

The stockmarket handed out several beatings to the company. The share price more than halved from a peak of 240p after some brokers took an unkind view of high debts and promotional spending at the fledgling plc.

At this time Kate had to fall back on her combative nature and an open-minded attitude to handle the criticism. 'Anyone doing things innovative and different has to be big enough and strong enough to handle criticism. You have to take the rough with the smooth.'

The setbacks were not linked to her being chief execu-tive. She reckons that anyone in her position would 'ruffle feathers' of the more established healthcare companies.

'We are creating something that is part of very big changes in the way healthcare is provided in the UK. Up to now, there has been an NHS monopoly for 50 years. The criticism will go on, but you never change anything without going through hard times', she says.

In terms of being a woman at the head of the new enterprise her attitude is one of robust defiance. 'If I believe I can do something, the fact that I'm a woman won't stop me doing it. I don't expect people to be nicer, or gentler, to me because I am a woman.'

And on the role of women in the business world, she offers the advice: Never use your sex as an excuse for not achieving'.

Those who work with Kate say she is a good leader because her enthusiasm shines through. Very unusually for a company that went public, about 70 per cent to 80 per cent of the staff are women. Many have been recruited after first coming into contact with the boss during her medical career. Kate Bleasdale thinks she is good at identifying people and part of the 'extremely exciting' feeling of growing is, she says, linked to making sure staff grow with the company.

Kate looks for people who are 'open-minded, not worried about change. People who have the ability to respond quickly to new things.' As chief executive she encourages staff to put forward ideas and not to be afraid if they don't get taken up, or do not work immediately. She is said to have determination and stamina and the ability to get things right more often than wrong.

♀

By the middle of 1999, Kate's public company persona had been forced to disappear. The road that had made her Alternative Investment Market entrepreneur of the year ended when she headed a management buy-out of Sinclair Montrose worth £40 million. Coincidentally, this was exactly the same value at which her company had made its market debut.

This part of Kate's story illustrated that the City, had in part, been right. The highly ambitious plans for Medicentres could not come to fruition. All of the centres outside of London were closed to leave the concept still running at just five places – at Victoria, Waterloo and Euston stations and Oxford St and Poultry in the City. 'You don't flog a dead horse. Outside London, the country did not seem ready for them', says Kate. It also illustrated how there can be a downside to being worth millions in the City.

Kate Bleasdale remembers being affected by press criticism. 'Now it is nice not getting up at weekends and seeing your name in the papers.'

'I can concentrate a lot more on purely company business. Now we are not in the glare of publicity, there are less distractions, like having to visit City investors and try and keep them sweet.'

Kate says the Medicentres that remain attract around 1,000 people a week between them and they pay around £4 million a year for the services. They do well out of corporate contracts where companies offer private health as a perk.

'Medicentres are around 3 per cent of our overall business, but they were attracting 100 per cent of the publicity. I suppose that is inevitable when you are trying to be innovative', Kate reflects.

When Sinclair Montrose quit the stockmarket it changed its name to Match Group to reflect the name of its biggest nursing and doctor staff agencies. The Match agency has bases in 25 hospitals in the UK, while other agencies in the group have a presence on 35 High Streets. The chain of agencies had a turnover of around £120 million during 2000, Kate says. Also her inclination to introduce new ideas shone through again as she launched a 'recruitment cafe' in Oxford St to tap a market to offer relaxed surroundings to all kinds of job-seekers who wanted to use the Internet to find work.

Meanwhile, a whole raft of online medical advice businesses are growing up in which doctors never actually meet their patients, but offer diagnosis over the net.

Also, the government itself is acknowledging the shortfalls of the NHS and introducing NHS Direct, a telephone consultancy service offering advice and recommending possible courses of action. The government is also encouraging family doctors to hold surgeries in private pharmacy chains as part of new thinking in health provision. It all seems similar in many ways to Kate Bleasdale's idea of shaking up the country's health provision.

♀

Nicola Foulston is the fast lady who took the fast lane to the top. She also made a fast exit from City life, by retiring as a millionairess while only 32.

She became chief executive of the Brands Hatch racing circuit while still in her 20s. She grabbed control of the British motor racing industry and shook it out of its amateur complacency. But what surprised those followers of the aggressive and ambitious Nicola Foulston was the way she has 'retired' from the thrill of the chase of corporate life at a very tender young age.

It has been said of Nicola that when it comes to a deal she is always the first out of the pits. And she was certainly born into the competitive world of motorsport. She inherited a fortune from her business tycoon father John Foulston, who had first made his money in Atlantic Computers and then bought the Brands Hatch circuit to pursue his own personal passion for motor racing.

When John Foulston was tragically killed in a crash at Silverstone in 1987, Nicola inherited the Brands Hatch business and became chief executive a year later. At that time, Brands had lost out on the rights to stage the lucrative British Grand Prix. Over the next decade, she kept Brands alive by hiring it for use by amateur drivers and eventually her Brands Hatch Leisure, including three other race tracks, grew sufficiently to join the stockmarket.

Nicola, who had dropped out of university because 'it wasn't challenging enough', then embarked on the most ambitious-sounding plot ever in motor racing. She made an audacious deal to win back the British Grand Prix for her own Brands Hatch from the Silverstone circuit and also ended the days when British motor racing was controlled by the amateurish and private British Racing Drivers Club. 'This is about much more than just the ownership of Silverstone. It is about how British motorsport should be managed in the future', she said in launching a £43 million bid. Nicola Foulston has been called the 'Margaret Thatcher of her generation' because of her gung-ho ways. But what is interesting is why she as a women even contemplated taking on the male-dominated BRDC. It is because she is an entrepreneurial woman to whom the importance of correct marketing is second nature. She would say the sport should be led by marketeers, who have to listen to the fans. 'The BRDC is a club for members who are very traditional. It is difficult for them to understand we are in 1999 and some woman like me can be running a company', she said.

Having won her biggest prize, Nicola Foulston adopted the 'smash and grab' attitude towards the City when she stood down as chief executive of Brands Hatch Leisure and went to live in Europe with millions under her belt. 'It's her prerogative, and who can blame her', said her PA. But at the 'not very ripe old age of 32', who can say she won't be back for more laps in the business race.

♀

In the macho world of money, how many can say more than 90 per cent of their staff are women . . . and their firm is a success? Financial advice firm, Fiona Price & Partners, is unique in this way. When Fiona Price set up her business in 1988, she can remember her colleagues at the Independent Financial Adviser where she worked reacting with fits of laughter. 'I intuitively thought it timely, but my male colleagues at the time thought it hysterical', Fiona says about her breakaway to pioneer a firm for financial advice mainly for women. Presently, 30 of her 33 staff are women.

In the beginning, she started with an overdraft of ten thousand pounds. The firm has since grown to one that handles around 5,000 clients and is worth more than £1.5 million a year in fee income. Right now, Fiona Price & Partners is at the stage where it aims to take off dramatically. It has, in Fiona's words, gone through the hard slog of winning awareness in the financial market place and gained critical mass. In summer 2000, the firm had outgrown its offices in Covent Garden and moved to much bigger and plusher offices in Holborn. 'A lot more people have been approaching us for help than we could hope to see.' Where rents, rates and service charges had cost £70,000 the new offices will cost £200,000 a year.

Fiona's plans for the 'next step' mean she wants to double her staff and aim for fees worth £4 million within three years. Also, she wants to broaden out from the London base with a goal to franchise into four or five regional centres. Furthermore, she wants to broaden appeal of her advisers away from richer professional women to those who want more instant help on an Internet service.

Managing director Price says: 'In the past, women were not deemed desirable clients in the sense that they were not seen as the main decision makers. Then in the 1980s the financial community discovered new clients and there was increased awareness of financial matters by women, either by intention, or by default.' Fiona, 40, says her idea grew because 'male financial bastions can be intimidating in the UK, with use of hard sell tactics and jargon. Until, or when, men become better communicators, more empathetic and better listeners there will be a market for us', said Fiona, who has a Psychology degree and an MBA under her belt.

Fiona Price & Partners director, Donna Bradshaw, also recognises that women have a different outlook on investment matters. 'Men are short-termist and speculative, and think they know more about money than they actually do, whereas women actually know more than they think', she says. In general, women are less confident about investment at first and more risk averse. 'There is a "me hunter, you stay at home and cook dinner attitude" in men and women that lingers back to childhood', she adds. But today's younger, professional, women, who have worked hard for their money are blurring the edges between the sexual stereotypes on who controls the money.

At the outset the firm's aim was to 'take financial planning to Britain's business and professional woman'. Its business remains advising on a whole range of tax, investment and pension requirements as well as more personal advice on things like divorce settlements and wills. More than seven out of ten clients are women, but the male element has been growing.

Fiona Price & Partners aims to provide 'impartial advice' and backs this with a break from the traditional commission-dominated way such firms earn fees. Instead clients tend to pay fees of £150 an hour for face-to-face advice. In the next phase of growth, the firm will work in areas where the law has been changing, such as when spouses' pensions are allocated straight away on divorce. The new 'stakeholder pensions' are an example where Fiona sees that her firm needs to turn changes in the law into an opportunity. Fiona herself would also like to see breaks in mortgage payments for 'child breaks' when women give up work to have children.

We have seen from a survey by the research and information company, Experian, that female entrepreneurs have
a different attitude from male entrepreneurs in terms of
what they feel their main role in business life is. Basically,
job creation, rather than pure personal wealth creation.
And Fiona Price backs this up. She says her three core
objectives of profitability, providing the best possible
service and providing a challenging and fun career for staff
are all completely equal. 'Profits remain important, but we
also want to provide a service because our clients really
need it. Equally my staff are important because I want
everyone to be fulfilled', she says.

Fiona rowed for Wales for seven years and represented
her country in the 1986 Commonwealth Games. She owns
three horses and is keen on eventing and drag hunting and
has clearly got a competitive streak. Not surprisingly, she
enjoys saying: 'We've got the last laugh now'.

Fiona, who does not have a family of her own, says the
firm is 'a very important part of me. It has taught me a
huge amount about life, not just about business. I'm paid
OK, but not mega-bucks. I feel guilty whenever I take any
more because it eats money for the business and its needs.'

As we know, the business is at a take-off stage. But this
has not happened without Fiona suffering in a way that all
entrepreneurs will experience. Building the business from
scratch meant she became 'totally drained'. Drained by
what she calls the constant domination of her life by
thoughts of the business: 'eating, sleeping, breathing it'.

Fiona Price went through a period of 18 months or so
of what she called 'living in chaos' at this time when she
bought and renovated a house and when she went through
the break-up of her engagement.

She has always had another side, apart from pioneering
business woman. This ranges from media work and public
speaking and being a faith-healer and on the board of
the City University and being a professional mentor. This
period coincided with the period that many own-made

business people will reach if their business dream takes off to the extent it becomes a big success. Fiona as founder entrepreneur was wanting to try to groom successors and move on from being a very hands-on managing director to more of a chairman with room to fulfil herself and her desires in other ways. This in geographic terms meant she tended to work more from home, from her 'sanctuary' in Gloucestershire. Since, she recalls, she was not so fully involved in the sense of being the figure-head actually in the office day-to-day, staff motivation fell and staff turnover rose.

The business hit a trough of stagnation that was not overcome until Fiona could put herself fully behind the new business plan. She has now let go of the reins a little and appointed three directors and given the staff the carrot of a possible stake in ownership in the future: 'the business is now more energised'. Her fellow director, Donna Bradshaw, says 'there is a very different feel to the business'. Fiona Price & Partners even tempted so-called City superwoman Nicola Horlick to be a star guest at the firm's annual party for clients. Horlick, in that mainly female company, came across as someone who 'recognised her own strengths and weaknesses, who was very "focused" and someone who obviously "does not suffer fools".'

In 1999 Fiona Price herself was voted 'Businesswoman of the Year' by the Small Business Bureau. This neatly rounded off a decade of success since she was similarly feted by *Cosmopolitan* magazine when it recognised her potential with its 'Women of Tomorrow' award in 1990 for young entrepreneurs.

♀

Kathleen O'Donovan made history when she became the first woman to rise to become head of finances at a major British company in 1991 when she was made Finance Director at BTR at the age of 34.

Her company was then a FTSE heavyweight, having grown to become one of the most extensive industrial conglomerates in the world with interests spanning engineering, aerospace, the Dunlop–Slazenger tyres and sports goods business, motors and many more.

O'Donovan was later joined by Rosemary Thorne in a very select club of women at near the very top of FTSE index companies, but, as we know, Thorne has now quit as FD at Sainsbury's. Thorne's new role as FD at Bradford & Bingley is a big job, but the company is not big enough to be ranked in the FTSE league. Meanwhile, O'Donovan has stayed in post over a decade in which her company has expanded and contracted through a spate of billion pound deals and eventually merged with another leading engineering group, Siebe, and emerged with a new name as Invensys, but nevertheless is still a FTSE member.

She began making a name for herself at the Hawker Batteries business, where she was nicknamed 'bubbles' by accounts staff, and emerged as finance director after BTR set out on a rapid expansion trail in the 1990s with a contested takeover of aero engine maker Hawker Siddeley.

Her BTR business paid a heavy price for an overambitious expansion policy in the 1990s. By buying low margin businesses on the back of heavy borrowings in a policy of racing with the world's conglomerates to gain size, BTR set itself up for problems when the recession set in and interest rates took off.

O'Donovan has been called a 'winner' as BTR and Siebe managements were weeded out and thrown together after their merger deal in late 1998. By that time, BTR had been forced to embark on a mass sell-off. Asked about how she felt about the marriage with Siebe, she said: 'We have got rid of business with about £6 billion in sales. I was involved in BTR when it was one of the biggest industrial groups, when it was a £10 billion a year company. I feel excited, we've been through great changes.' Specialism in accounting and finance has been one of the best ways for women to break through. There is a belief that women in these areas are able to rise faster because, in dealing with bald financial facts, it is easier to make an objective assessment of performance.

Those who have worked with Kathleen O'Donovan say she 'is renowned for having a head for juggling assets, but is less good at having flair for handling people and an intuition for new opportunities'. Traditionally, being a finance director has been a platform to break through to the very top and move into a chief executive's chair. O'Donovan has a £400,000 salary package and non-executive directorships at EMI and the Bank of England. Having had nearly a decade close to the top she needs to show more charisma to stand a chance of being the first woman FTSE company boss.

Other women have found that the best route to the boardroom has been via a mastery of figures and use of the calculator.

For Elizabeth Airey these skills and others picked up as a former stockbroking oils analyst were useful as she rose to be finance director at Monument Oil and Gas. But what got her into the ultimate 'no lose' situation and landed a £3 million financial jackpot was literally 'sleeping with the enemy'. Elizabeth, 40, was finance director while her partner was in the same role at rival oil group Lasmo while Lasmo mounted a successful takeover bid for the smaller Monument Oil in 1999.

Wendy Smyth was finance director at Saatchi and Saatchi in the days when it became one of the most famous, and largest, advertising agencies in the world. Smyth was the first female director ever at Saatchis. She also proved she had a strong personality by standing up and being counted against the founding brothers, Maurice and Charles, and was an influential figure as Saatchi and Saatchi was reformed with a break-away agency called Cordiant and the remaining half of the business sold to Publicis for £1.2 billion. She has been praised for her 'very brave' stance against Maurice Saatchi and at 46 she still has time on her hands to climb higher.

Mastering the way City financial markets behave has also provided a launch pad for entrepreneurial women. Janie Dear had a 15-year career as a specialist in European equities, working for big name banks like Kleinwort Benson and BZW in big cities like New York and Hong Kong, before returning home to wave goodbye to that lifestyle and finding her own 'Soup Opera' chain of food outlets. Janie Dear remembers New York's 'real can-do attitude' and its more welcoming environment for start-up businesses. 'Sometimes people in the UK are too shy about admitting they want to make a bit of money', she feels. Don't rule out her business being traded on its own merits in the City.

# 12

## *Sex in the City*

Male dominance in the world of money has lasted for centuries. But in the City today, two women, Nicola Horlick and Carol Galley, have risen to the very top. They, between them, head two of the most powerful City investment firms. More than this, one of them, Nicola Horlick has become a household name in her own right. A most unusual occurrence given the anonymous, faceless and generally staid way in which the City's power brokers have traditionally gone about their business. Carol Galley has stood out because of the power she has exerted in influencing the greatest takeover battles in our age. It is because she is a woman in an environment that has been ruled for so long by men that she is the focus of attention.

Furthermore, the City has been bedevilled by an image of being one of the most sexist environments in which to work. We will deal with how the big institutions and banks have lost a string of sexual harassment cases. Also we will see how the City has been trying to open up and change its ways. Whether or not this will open up new opportunities for top women will be interesting to watch. Presently, it just shines the spotlight even more brightly on the likes of Nicola Horlick and Carol Galley.

First, we are interested in what makes Nicola Horlick who she is.

What is it that enabled her to stand out in the male dominated environment in the first place? And why did she
choose to return to City work every time after having five
children when many others have opted for a quieter life at
home?

♀

Nicola Horlick first made her name as the young woman
who rose fast to head Deutsche Morgan Grenfell's
£18 billion pension fund business.

Her career, throughout the 1980s and early 1990s, to
head the business at the tender age of 35 was remarkable
in a merchant bank that had been, in the 'old city', the
epitome of male-dominated blue-blooded institutions.

Nicola Horlick had earned the tag of city 'superwoman'
by earning millions in bonuses because of her investment
performance which had been beating most of the performance achieved by the men. But she earned the tag also
because she earned pathos. It was Nicola who took on so
much at work while her daughter, the eldest of five children under the age of 11, was dying of leukaemia. And it
was Nicola who, in 1997, was sacked by Morgan Grenfell
for 'disloyalty' at a time when this leukaemia was really
taking hold of her daughter, Georgie. Nicola is married to
Tim Horlick, who himself earned millions as head of corporate finance at Salomon Brothers. She quite patently didn't
need to work to earn money. Nevertheless, she caught
the public eye and gained public sympathy because of the
way in which she displayed great chutzpah in storming off
to the bank's headquarters in Frankfurt to demand to be
reinstated.

The bank wanted to sack her because they alleged disloyalty in the form of a supposed plot by Horlick to defect
with her team to a rival ABN Amro. 'I was motivated by a

strong sense of injustice. I had stuck with Morgan Grenfell in very difficult circumstances', Nicola said.

Whatever the rights or wrongs, the manner in which Horlick reacted defined her place in public mythology and lowered her esteem in the eyes of the stuffy City elite in equal measure. Nicola was no longer a figure who ordinary people could not identify with. The show woman side of her took over from the cool, calculating dealer. Nicola had, after all, once auditioned for the Royal Academy of Dramatic Arts and set up a theatre group while at Oxford. And this confidence in self-presentation is something that no man or woman who reaches near the top in the City can be altogether lacking. Bluff and bonds are never that far apart. Nicola went, with a string of pearls round her neck and a string of journalists in tow, to Frankfurt without a care that her actions could be called hysterical. She was described at the time as a kind of 'Mrs Tiggywinkle with an outboard motor' because of her bustling, bossy, 'get my own way no matter what' manner.

The City old school remarked that once she became a public spectacle it would be the end of her reputation and it was even claimed she put back the cause of women in general in the City by 20 years. However, the truth was that much of the City already disliked her purely out of jealousy. Simply because she was a woman who earned lots of money and who had been eating into their patch.

Nicola has said about being suspended from her career at Morgan Grenfell that she felt 'cornered'. Also she has interesting thoughts on how she, as a top woman, reacted differently to a top man in the same situation. 'It is quite a female thing, when something is not fair, to stand out and say so. More of a manly reaction would be to shrug shoulders and get on with life.'

Her case against Morgan Grenfell did fizzle out, but before long she was back in the big time when she launched a fund management business from scratch for the French bank Société Générale. A job for which she once again is rewarded handsomely with a salary of more than half a million a year. When Nicola landed the new job she still had five children. Her daughter Georgie finally died in late 1998. The new role at Société Générale would require incredible effort and the decision to take it on would have looked wrong in the eyes of many young mothers. But Nicola was in no doubt. 'I went back because I needed to show them I wasn't going to be pushed out of the City just like that', she said in an interview at the time.

Nicola says about the sex battle in the City: 'I do think everybody should have equal opportunity. Except that we have to have the children. If you don't have children you are on a level playing field with the men.' When pressed though, she does concede she was very lucky in having two 'extremely enlightened' bosses when she was having her own family. We shall explore exactly what was it about Nicola and what she did to seemingly 'have it all' later.

The decision of Nicola to go on working while her daughter was terminally ill is another thing that seems curious to many people.

Nicola Horlick, in her own autobiography *Can You Really Have It All?* explained that she took some kind of inspiration from her daughter Georgie who had urged her to carry on because she knew her mother would only be 'bored' if she stopped. More poignant was Georgie's wish to pack in as much as she could while she could. In turn, it dawned on Nicola that she herself might only have a short while to 'make a mark on the world' and so she had to make as much money as she could. The trait in personality that had always been part of Nicola's make-up was the desire to 'pack every minute'. The desire to do everything, non-stop.

This desire is alien to the vast majority of people. Nicola has explained it in terms of using work as an 'escape mechanism', a means where she would keep working longer than might otherwise have been the case to try and lead as normal a life as possible. 'I have to accept that I probably have more energy than most people. I was born hyper-active. I generally go to sleep at about 12.30 and wake up at about 6.30 and like to pack as much as possible into every minute of the day', Nicola once revealed in an interview. This explains something about the 'superwoman'. Equally revealing is the admission, a few months after Georgie died, that Nicola worked 'largely to keep me sane' and she felt, by extension, that if she kept sane her family would always be okay.

♀

The sheer determination, force of personality and rebellious streak that sets Nicola apart today were characteristics that she showed from a very early age.

She grew up in a well-off setting in the Wirral, Cheshire, with a businessman father and a mother who had fled Poland when the Germans entered Warsaw in 1939 and who obviously passed on a penchant for hard work. In an interview for the *Daily Telegraph*, Nicola said of her mother, Suzanna Gayford, 'she was a housewife by day and studied architecture by night. She looked permanently exhausted yet she managed to do everything well.' Nicola inherited her mother's work ethic and energy. This meant she, aged just five, decided her girls' school was too 'pathetic' and insisted she be transferred to her brother's prep school. Aged 11 her good brain was apparent and she was sent to one of the country's foremost girls' public schools, Cheltenham Ladies' College. Here her desire to stand out was manifest. She is said to have hated the place because she was only one of a thousand girls.

Nicola recollects feeling that boys were more straight-forward and less bitchy than girls of her age. She also didn't like the unfairness of being fed measly portions at meal times.

In any event, Nicola, aged 14, decided to run away. This she did and she got as far as Cheltenham railway station before being stopped by the police. But even this did not seem to faze her. An 'indomitable sense of her rightness' that is remarked upon by those she comes into contact with in the City was apparent. She refused to give her name to the police, asked them for proof of a search warrant when they wanted to find out who she was by looking into her handbag and was furious they had stopped her going home.

Nicola's parents took the view she had ruined her chance for a good education, but they were to be proved wrong. Nicola talked her own way into a place at Birkenhead High School by phoning up the headmistress. There her academic prowess meant she passed four 'A' levels. In particular, Maths came very easy and it was a subject in which she never really had to try and this showed the seeds of a mind that was later having to juggle billions in the City.

From school Nicola went on to Balliol college, Oxford, to read Law. Here she was one of 30 women in a college of 500 men and was able to enjoy the attention. Here she also met her future husband Tim. In him she saw someone who could be an equal sparring partner, whereas previous boyfriends had been easy to push around and had done what she told them.

Nicola at university also showed signs of the high energy lifestyle that she carries on to this day and she 'filled every minute with some kind of activity'.

Nicola was president of the Oxford Law Society. Also she set up her own drama society and a tale from these days is revealing. When it put on a production of *The Crucible*, Nicola was the director and in true student fashion was also involved in the costume-making. But she also became leading lady when her original choice for the star part was 'insufficiently passionate'.

She later conceded she might have taken on too much. But the incident showed the desire to be in control of everything that has become apparent in her City life. Also when she was later applying for RADA she was known for the great lengths she would take to get the part and the thoroughness of her research. Traits that once again would be needed for doing the business in fund management.

♀

Those who worked on the same team with Nicola at Morgan Grenfell say she was herself a wonderful boss in that she would act as any mother would. She would soothe them, reward them and discipline them. The hard streak would show through when Nicola was assembling people around her. 'I was ruthless in the sense of team-building – that if someone doesn't fit, I decided they shouldn't be there', she said.

Nicola describes her management style as being like a 'mother hen' figure. She pinpoints characteristics like being protective and being good at listening that add up to the use of very strong maternal instincts in her style. Horlick is also critical of those women who try to suppress their feminine characteristics in favour of male ones once they get into leadership positions. She also recalls how she was 'intensely irritated' when she saw discrepancies in pay for men and women doing the same job. At Morgan Grenfell she saw there were quite a lot of these anomalies and she made sure they were ironed out.

♀

Nicola Horlick is famously one who pays great attention to detail.

This fastidiousness even applied when it came to her own pregnancies. Nicola, we have gathered is someone who feels work is an overwhelmingly important part of her life. She believes also that it is the right instinct for women to let their maternal feelings loose and have children. Nicola might even say women who choose not to have children in order to pursue their careers are in some ways selfish. Combining the two roles has required planning and Nicola says she planned each of her babies to arrive at the end of the year in December, when the City is at its least busy with company news and deals. This was because she 'could take maternity leave over Christmas.'

Nicola claims it is something of a myth that surrounded her that she spent the whole time in the office and she does claim to have taken 'full maternity leave'. But, Nicola herself was born on 28 December, and perhaps, one feels, should have known better. The City high-flier explains her 'calculating' attitude to contraception by saying: 'I am just very lucky. I have a perfect 28-day cycle. I know precisely when I am ovulating.'

Other tales of Horlick and her children point to her own dedication and to the importance of two other links in her family life – her husband and her nanny. When Nicola was pregnant with her second child, Alice, she did not give up work until the day she was due and Nicola was reportedly 'very cross' when the innocent babe actually appeared nine days late. Also when Georgie was at one stage pulled back from death's door Nicola went back to work within a couple of days. 'I simply had to do it. I have had split loyalties throughout my life. I have my work and my team and I also have my husband and my children. I just can't forget one at the expense of the other', she said at that time.

The first pillar in Nicola's life is husband Tim and the pair of them have been together for twenty or so years. However, no matter what Nicola earns herself, she is deferential to him and takes the 'very traditional' attitude that it is up to her to run house and home. The other take on this is that it is another example of her not being totally happy unless she is in total control. Another important pillar has been Nicola's ever-reliable nanny Joan Buckfield who had been with the family for nine years already when Nicola had her shocks of losing one job and one of her childen. 'I had the same nanny for so long that the children were happy with the situation. That was a deciding factor – the most important thing is that they are happy', Nicola said in a BBC radio interview.

But, these essential pillars for Nicola do not in themselves unlock the key to her success. As we shall see with the examples of other women who have reached near the top in the business world, unbelievably high salaries can buy you any amount of support you need. However, this wealth and support does not always lead to the necessary happiness to make a top woman stay in the City.

For Nicola, we have to look at her intelligence that needs stimulating, her desire to be constantly fulfilled and her competitive spirit that means she does not get trodden upon. Also, she has the capacity to keep many more things juggling away in her head than is the case with most people. 'I'm a planner, I have to think months ahead', she once said. We also have to acknowledge her very great determination. 'If you are going to succeed in life you need to be determined. If you are not, and you are just a wimp and let people walk all over you, you're never going to get anywhere', she said.

Nicola Horlick obviously has a great courageous streak as well. We saw this while she took on the City establishment. Also, she spent months following the death of her daughter to use her high-profile name to promote the Leuka 2000 charity which raised money to research the disease.

As to being an adequate role-model for other women high-achievers, that is open to doubt. Nicola herself is a staunch believer in 'a more meritocratic world' and says this choice is there for the taking. But, Nicola Horlick is a formidable woman. A unique and formidable woman, and as such, not someone who can be copied.

♀

Nicola is not alone in succeeding in business and having a family. But she is unusual in reaching the very top of the City and continuing to run a large family.

There have been others who were so attached to their job that they never really let childbirth deflect them from climbing the career ladder. Take the amazing tale of Sue Clark, who was called one of the brightest young talents of Scottish commerce and who rose to be director of corporate affairs at Railtrack in her mid-30s. Sue hit the headlines when she was PR chief of Scottish Power defending a £4.5 billion bid against Pacificorp by staying at her desk even after her waters had broken and contractions had begun when she was just about to have her daughter Lucy.

But most women top executives do not stay put when a family arrives. Louise Rouswell was a high flying commodities broker at Salomon Bros who found the City demanding but stimulating. She tried returning to work for three days a week after the birth of her first child but found it 'sappingly tiring' and when she subsequently had twins she ended her career at just 36. 'If there was a chink of light in your armour, someone else wanted to exploit it and leap into your seat – particularly if you were female. Because it tends to be a more male life, it becomes a happier place for a man to work', she said.

The decision of Penny Hughes to quit when she was at the pinnacle of her career at Coca-Cola at the age of 35 caused a welter of publicity.

Penny Hughes, who was earning £250,000 as president of Coca-Cola UK, echoed a decision made by Brenda Barnes who quit as head of Pepsi's North American division in favour of her family of three. Penny's decision, apart from the press interest, even brought accusations that it set back the image of women in management.

Penny had all the credentials to reach the top. She was head girl at her school in Merseyside, went on to get a first in chemistry at Sheffield University, and had self-confidence in abundance. She is the type of person who can't really understand why other people have to struggle, or understand why they might find life difficult. She became boss of Coke at just 33. What is strange about her decision to quit after just two years at the top is that Penny was a big fan of women in work and also that she obviously enjoyed using her power to influence a whole change in climate. 'To try and run a business by ignoring a very valuable portion of the workforce is crazy', she would say. Also she claimed she 'was never too busy' in the sense that she had to stay at her job long into the night in the way that, for instance, solicitors seem to do on a very regular basis.

Penny lived by not taking work home and by leaving by 6 p.m. Also she would not promote people who had to work 12 hours a day on the basis they were 'obviously not up to it'. 'I was surprised at the kerfuffle when I resigned, but Coke is the world's largest brand and I was the youngest and only female president they ever had', she said.

Her decision to leave a fantastic job was a classic case of trying to weigh the biological clock for a thirty-something female and the thrills of corporate power. Penny explained: 'I had meant to have children in my early 30s, then at 33 I was promoted to president. By the time I was 35, I had been in the ultimate leadership position at Coke in the UK for two years and I thought "I had to have children now". I didn't want my children to arrive and then be passed off to somebody else. I had had a great start in life due to my mum and I wanted to give my children the same stability.'

She too had interesting opinions on the female qualities of being a boss, saying 'her team' at work needed mentoring and day-to-day handling and this was not going to be possible from her in a part-time way. Hughes admitted that she thought she could 'do the brain part of the job' while having a family, but 'not the emotional part, the managerial part of running the company'. 'The thrills of multi-million pound corporate decision-making didn't compare with the thrills of a first baby', she found. Also her next promotion would have been abroad to run an even bigger country for Coke and she preferred the 'patriotic' idea of staying in the UK and providing a stable environment for children and then returning to consultancies and directorships at a later date.

Penny Hughes has tiptoed back into the business world with non-executive directorships and some well-paid consultancy and speech-making jobs. However, her feelings about juggling business life provide contrast to the likes of Nicola Horlick who maintained a drive and passion for staying involved alongside having a family.

However, things are changing since 1993 when Penny Hughes caused that stir of publicity by chucking things in. She says, the new century is heralding a new culture. It now no longer causes such offence when people do business from home. The so-called concept of portfolio careers is changing things and Penny Hughes hopes this will benefit men as well as women. 'They can benefit from the new flexibility too.'

In her own way, Penny Hughes could have done more to break old business conventions by quitting than she first envisaged.

♀

The City world has a bad reputation when it comes to women. In the few decades since women began to work alongside men in the Square Mile, sexual harassment cases have been plentiful.

In an unfortunate irony of a world that hates to lose money, City banks and institutions on both sides of the

Atlantic have had to pay out millions of pounds in compensation cases for sexism.

Against this background, the career of Carol Galley stands out. She has been able to rise to be dubbed the 'Queen of the City' and head a fund management business that controls a money mountain approaching £400 billion.

Carol Galley has been one of the most powerful players in shaping corporate life. In her leading position at Mercury Asset Management her firm had a decisive influence on the way Granada won control of the Forte hotels and restaurants empire in what was one of the most hotly-contested battles of the 1990s.

Since 1997, Galley's MAM has been owned by the huge US bank, Merrill Lynch. Galley, as co-chairman of the investment management business with her long-standing partner Stephen Zimmerman, is able to command a salary and bonus package worth £3 million.

The duo have a 29-year career as an investment partnership in which they became the most famous double act in fund management. Direct involvement in wheeler-dealing took a back seat as Merrill Lynch internationalised a business that has 3,500 staff in 21 countries around the world. Galley and Zimmerman announced that they will leave Merrill Lynch in the year 2001.

Carol Galley has been called an 'ice maiden' because of her cool, detached and secretive manner as she climbed to the top in the City. However, she does have views about her management role which are worth exploring, though first we need to see how she made it despite male domination of the City.

The fund management queen of today had her roots in a thirst for knowledge. Galley, now 51, read modern languages at Leicester University after schooldays in a grammar school in Gosforth. Though language skills would undoubtedly be beneficial in the increasingly international City life, it was the passion for research that really set Carol on her way.

She began humbly in the library of Warburgs in the days when it was a grand old name and an independent merchant bank. But what set Carol apart from other librarians was her desire to take a deep interest in any material she was asked to pick out for investment analysts. It is recalled that she would not merely look out annual company reports when requested, but have the 'disquieting habit of reading, digesting and interpreting them'. These inclinations and talents were recognised and she was promoted into the business end of banking life and joined Warburg's MAM operation.

By 1987 Carol was made head of MAM's pension fund business in the UK and from this position she started building the reputation as one of the most powerful people in the City. The ability to assimilate great streams of information, the attention to detail, the instincts about financial trends and the cool detachment were all attributes she needed as she decided the fate of some of the biggest companies in Britain.

What brought the press-shy Galley into the public eye and made her reputation in the City was the way her MAM business first used its buying power, built from managing people's pension money and savings, to help Granada win Forte. Galley's MAM controlled 11 per cent of the shares in Sir Rocco Forte's group and it was her decision to vote in favour of the hostile £4 billion takeover bid from the Granada media and leisure empire that swung the contest in Granada's favour and saw Granada win control of prize names like the Savoy Hotel and Claridge's. Galley's investment firm also played a key role in re-shaping the 1990s commercial TV sector when it voted in favour of Granada in its takeover of London Weekend TV.

Her style has been likened to a religious fervour in the way she invests millions and she was once quoted as saying that wasting money was 'a sin'.

Galley, aged 53, has avoided being written about in the press and in truth, her private life, with no children from her marriage to a German stockbroker, seems uneventful. With only occasional relaxation in a cottage in the South of France and a mansion in Belgravia as diversions she could be the typical 'super-rich, time-poor' city workaholic.

Anyone in Carol's position, over a span of nearly three decades, cannot hope to call the markets right all the time and she has seen an 'unhappy period of performance' lately when her investment managers appeared too conservative and missed out on the late 1990s techno-boom. Galley and Merrill Lynch were even having to face a compensation claim on supposed investment shortfall from her clients the Unilever pension fund.

Carol says: 'I've always wanted to be a leader of a team and play a leadership role, but it is the team that is important'. Zimmerman and herself moved more into people management rather than pure fund management. 'It is quite difficult. One of the hardest things is letting go. But you have to do it', Galley said in an interview with the *Mail on Sunday* in 2000. In this sentiment she would be sharing the feelings experienced by many of the entrepreneurs she has put an investment price upon in the past.

The disastrous way senior partners of City broking houses in the past have wasted millions by poor management should be a warning. Galley, in her staff, also has a highly trained team in the art of analysing the worth of bosses and a team that is used to giving the thumbs-up, or thumbs-down, to whole groups of companies on the basis of an impression made by their directors.

Carol Galley hints at how softer 'woman's skills' can be useful even in the hitherto macho world of money. She feels markets are not best analysed purely in terms of facts and statistics. 'Sentiment and emotion are critical, so your team needs to include people who have a feel for sentiment', she said. Galley adds that it is not always appropriate to be completely logical because you are always dealing with human faults and frailties and that is, for her, the exciting part of the job.

It remains to be seen if Galley will make a City come-back. But her legacy in paving the way for the likes of Katherine Garrett-Cox, who at 33 was made head of Aberdeen Asset Management, is there for all to see.

♀

Tales from the City on how the men have reacted to the arrival of 'the skirts' in the Square Mile vary from the funny to the very sad, depending on your standpoint.

For instance, the year in the mid-1990s when Deutsche Morgan Grenfell realised it was so underweight in women that its Christmas party for staff and clients would have gone flat. Deutsche's solution was to ship in 40 women from the Midlands hired at £150 each from an entertain-ment agency for the night to mingle with the bank's corporate guests. The 'extra' female staff were hired to help the evening go with a bang, but they were not prostitutes, said the bank. The agency said: 'They want our girls to do a bit of schmoozing and talking to the bald, fat, bloke in the corner. It is often very senior executives who don't know many people and are left standing alone and that is obviously very embarrassing.' The actual staff, as you might expect, were not amused. 'We were told they were hired for the night because it was a very male-dominated event and the company didn't have many female bankers. They stood out like a sore thumb. All us female bankers were dressed quite sensibly and these girls were dressed very revealingly', said one member.

♀

Dancing instructor-turned-business woman, Debbie Moore, made history in 1982 when she floated her Pineapple Dance studio company and appeared on the old stock exchange trading floor in a leotard and became the first woman company chairman to tread that particular floor. She said about her experience at the time: 'people thought I was this tough, high-flying, aggressive type but I am not like that at all'. And she went on to say she was typical of women bosses who scored higher in 'emotional intelligence' than male bosses and she reckoned she was where she was because she had used strengths such as empathy with staff and knew how to let them express their emotions.

The first women were allowed on the old Stock Exchange trading floor in the late 1970s. They were met with teasing and the odd 'raucous reception', as were young male blue-button trainees. This reception was accepted as being part of the learning process, especially in the days when market-makers needed to get to know and trust their counterparts.

♀

But, the City firms were wrong to allow male employees to exploit, harass and discriminate against women for so long. And it was not until the 1990s that women began to fight back.

'Power play is so much part of the City culture', re-marked Helena Dennison from the City Women's Net-work. Opportunity Now says: 'The culture of the City has a long way to go, especially at senior levels. It is way behind most other sectors.'

On one level, women were so rare in City dealing rooms that they attracted attention and were subject to degrading crude jokes, had to put up with strippagrams for their male colleagues, and were even driven out because of the sexual bullying and advances. There have been rare examples of women coming to the top in the City. Bronwyn Curtis stood out by becoming chief economist at Nomura, a Japanese investment bank that shared the bad reputation of banks from that culture that were notorious for their hostility to women. Curtis later used her experiences to land the job of being managing director for Bloombergs TV and Radio side in Europe. 'The climate is getting better than when I started in the City in 1987, but I don't think you'll see drastic changes in the next five years. Maybe in the next 10 or so but, it will take a new generation of men to change it', she says.

Because bosses at City firms were overwhelmingly men who had advanced through this culture themselves, women often came up against a brick wall when trying to make internal complaints. This led a brave few to risk their reputations and go to the courts. The past decade has seen such cases well-reported and extensively reported in the press and it needn't concern this book to go into all of them again. Suffice it to briefly mention the highest profile ones and then look at the case of Aisling Sykes because this has interesting implications in whether or not the 'horrendously long hours culture' can ever be broken down.

In 1993, sexism in the City world hit the headlines when City insurance broking firm Willis Corroon lost a sexual discrimination case against a young female employee, Samantha Phillips, 28, who had been sacked. Phillips claimed she had been the victim of a male conspiracy to get rid of her after she had rejected sexual advances from her superior, Giles Wilkinson, and been branded as a 'bimbo' while they were both abroad on a business trip to Copenhagen. She was awarded £18,000 after a tribunal said any male colleague would not have been sacked in the same way.

Then more recently in 1999 Kay Swinburne took on and won her case against Deutsche Bank after she alleged she had been 'driven out' of her £300,000 a year job as a senior investment banker because her own official complaints about sexual innuendos were not being taken seriously by her bosses. The case was dubbed a modern day case of 'David versus Goliath' as Deutsche was at the time the biggest bank in the world and it spent at least half a million pounds fielding a team of a dozen lawyers against her. It was felt the case could open the floodgates for a stream of others from disgruntled females in the 'testosterone-driven' Square Mile.

Aisling Sykes decided to fight one of the biggest names in the City on the battleground of time. More precisely: How much time does your employee own of your life?, no matter how many hundreds of thousands you are paid by them.

Sykes, aged 39, was a vice-president at J. P. Morgan and had risen rapidly despite the handicap of having a family of three. During her seven years with J. P. Morgan, she told of how she would be expected to work 14-hour days, and of fielding calls from places like Tokyo at midnight at her home.

When she was pregnant with her fourth child, she decided she had had enough of 'having a phone on one arm and a new baby on the other' and she asked J. P. Morgan if she could work more flexible hours. Sykes was sacked in 1998, because, she says, the bank were not prepared to be flexible and allow her to be at home 'to spend a little time with the children while they were awake'. Sykes also said she was in such a specialist position that the option of a career break was not a real one and she would never have been able to climb back up the career ladder. Sykes was handsomely paid, with a basic salary of £70,000 with bonuses to come. She won a £12,000 unfair dismissal award two years later, but the tribunal did say that her salary meant she could well afford to pay nannies and refused her claim that J. P. Morgan's refusal to allow flexible working amounted to indirect sexual discrimination. Having tried to juggle three children and a very tough job Sykes says the lesson to be drawn is: 'To succeed as a top woman in the City, you either have to choose not to have children, or be adamantly prepared to put the job first no matter what'.

♀

There can be no doubt that there are also advantages to being female in the world of finance. In the days when women were rare in decision-making positions in City broking houses, any who were any good would stand out and gain the chance to be promoted faster than their male colleagues.

The way in which Karren Brady was made managing director of Birmingham City, the football club that also floated as a business on the stock market, at the incredibly young age of 23 certainly raised eyebrows.

Brady had been selling advertising at the *Sunday Sport* newspaper owned by David Sullivan and she had a very good relationship with him as boss. When Sullivan bought Birmingham in 1993, Brady was installed as the MD. Brady added to her colourful profile by later marrying one of her club's strikers, Paul Peshisolido. She then became the first corporate executive to claim the 'honour' of saying they had sold her husband, when Brady agreed to sell him to Fulham.

A Reuters survey in autumn 2000 found that City institutions appeared to be more sensitive. However the motivation for this new found sensitivity could be coming from the wrong source, the survey hinted. 'Banks feel they are obliged to react, not necessarily because they think something is wrong but because they could get sued.'

New sensitivity to sexism is applauded. New technology and new attitudes have arrived to make flexible working more acceptable than was the case even a few years ago when Aisling Sykes was caught in the work versus family trap. How long will it take the City to realise it might make more money by being enlightened enough to hold on to its top staff? Or do banks have to lose a lot more money yet in the courts?

# 13

# *A Question of Balance*

Karen Jones stands out from all other bar-goers – she tends to own them, or manage them. Since the 1980s she has been the driving force behind so-called 'theme bars' in the UK. Karen Jones built up the Café Rouge and Dome chains from small beginnings of one restaurant in 1989 to a business that was worth £133 million seven years later.

During her 20s and 30s, Karen advanced her reputation and reached the top and did so while also having three children. Well-known as an incredibly hard worker, Karen's personal story provides insight into the way entrepreneurs achieve their goals. Also we learn from her how she seemingly manages to have it all and how being 'number one' makes this easier and possible.

Jan Hall is another woman who has made it to the top while also having a family. As chief executive of one of the largest advertising agencies in Europe she ran a staff of 1,000. She has fascinating insights about her dual roles as boss of the firm and the family. Jan has since become a senior headhunter, become a director at public companies and continued in senior roles at influential business organisations and later we will learn her views on how the business climate for women is going.

Despite a family, and having made a fortune already, Karen Jones is so in love with the bar and restaurant world that she is heading a new challenge in the food and drink business. Karen is now chief executive of Punch Retail, the managed chains side of Punch Taverns' pub and restaurant empire. As boss of this business, Karen took control of the 1,060 managed public houses bought from Allied Domecq in October 1999 and she is heading the Bar Room Bar chain as it expands outside its London base to cities like Birmingham and Leeds. Also the company has been opening new brands such as Big Steak Pub, Wacky Warehouse and Mr Q's and introduced a number of new, trial concepts.

With these new bars, Karen is taking theme bars into a different era. While the 140 or so Cafés Rouges and the Dome bars were growing so successfully they could all be identified by being more chic and sophisticated than the competition. The decor and the ambience caught the imagination of those who wanted more than just food or drink.

The main common thread for her new projects is going to be value for money. Chief Executive Karen Jones said: 'One of the main challenges is to make the large number of small unbranded local pubs within our estate really work for us. Rather than adopt the overt, mass branding route, our philosophy will be to treat each pub as an individual outlet and do what is right for that pub in its location.'

'I strive for excellence and try and inject into my own establishments what I would personally go out for. I'm tired of spending 50 quid on nothing', Karen said. Equally important is the need to serve the contemporary customer, who has money, high tastes, but not much time. Karen has recognised a market for those who want West End-style entertainment, but on their own home ground.

In the Bar Room Bars these 'extras' range from art exhibitions in the Battersea bar to a resident DJ at Kennington, but according to Karen they all, at the minimum, are: 'Great bars with fabulous pizza'. 'Niche concepts are the way of the future because the beer market is flat', she thinks.

Karen Jones, when asked about the secret of her success, says: 'Most people are at heart an operator, or a financier. I'm very much an operator. I genuinely love being in the business I'm in. There is nothing to beat the buzz of going into your own bar and seeing it packed.'

Indeed Karen started out by being a waitress in one of the first theme bars in London, Peppermint Park, while in her first career out of university – advertising. Karen, who got a first in English and US Literature from East Anglia University, said she loved the intellectual side of advertising. 'But in the end I didn't want to be a cog in the wheel. I realised I wanted to call the shots. I wanted it to be my vision and wasn't going to be happy with anyone else interfering. I wanted to be an entrepreneur rather than a good corporate player', Karen said.

So she took the difficult decision to chuck an advertising career and start out on the road with partner Roger Myers in restaurants. She became operations director of this first business, then in 1989, co-founded the Pelican Group which was the quoted company for the Café Rouge and Dome chains. Karen was managing director by the time Pelican was sold to Whitbread in 1996 in a deal that made her about three million pounds. All the while, Karen had the reputation of being a very 'hands-on' boss. 'I love serving people and making them happy.' And to this day she returns to her bars most evenings after putting her three children to bed.

'The bar and restaurant business is an addictive world. It takes quite a lot to beat seeing one of your own places taking off and doing well', she said.

Speaking about the time when Whitbread took over the Pelican business Karen says: 'It was a natural progression. They were a good cultural fit and provided the financial muscle'. Karen, 40, claims to have 'an opportunistic outlook' and said she started Café Rouge with the aim of selling after the chain grew to eight. She stayed with the business under Whitbread until 1998. But she likes 'lean, flat management structures' and her entrepreneurial nature could not be held back for long.

♀

By many people's yardsticks Karen can be called a workaholic. She recalls going back to work just five days after the birth of her daughter. 'Without question it is easier to be your own boss.' This means she could take her new child into work and breastfeed in most extraordinary places and get away with it. 'Liquor rooms, rubbish rooms and anywhere I could find. I can't imagine being able to do that if it wasn't my own company', she says. She could work hard, but on her own terms. She also acknowledges the benefits of a very decent salary and of being able to afford lots of help. 'Of course there are stresses and strains, but the spotlight should not be on me but on women who are supporting a family on relatively low income', she thinks.

'When you run your own company, you drive yourself because you want to, not because you have to. There is, in a sense, no cut off point and your company and your home life flow together', says Karen.

Asked why she took on the challenges of launching a new business at the same time as having a family, Karen said: 'I started my own business so that when the point came when I was having children, although I was working very hard, I could work those hours to suit me.'

Karen Jones has been lucky, for example keeping the same nanny for nine years. 'Without my team – at home and at work – it would not be possible. They really are a secret weapon.' Karen says she would have found life worrying and uncomfortable if things had been the other way around and she was a mere employee. 'I would have been worrying about whether the boss could allow time off. I would resent meetings eating into family time.' This is revealing about what women entrepreneurs, who reach the top, think about priorities in their lives.

Karen has also experienced the 'let down' period experienced by many entrepreneurs when the time comes to move a step back and become less operational. For her this was in 1993 when the business had grown so it needed a proper management structure. 'This meant I had to stop running around and doing everything and interfering madly. This was becoming less effective because I had less time. I found that really painful, but it is unrealistic to expect a company to stay the same. It has to mutate.'

However, for Karen Jones, behind it all is a passion for the restaurant business: 'I crave involvement'. She likes being active in the business world. Her other roles include being on the board of the National Theatre and a non-executive director of publisher EMAP.

♀

A track record in climbing to the top of businesses gives Jan Hall a respected voice on the subject of women in the world of work. In her first career in advertising Jan rose to become the European Chief Executive of the GGT Group plc. With overall profit responsibility for all activities of the 17 European companies in the group that is one of the top handful of agency groups in the world, she was in charge of nearly 1,000 staff.

As Jan herself describes it: 'Some still measure success in terms of turnover, size of business and the number of people they control. The "big cheese" is being the general manager, as a finance director, for instance, you don't have to run people in the same way.'

After being a 'big cheese' in the communications world, Jan Hall moved in 1997 to become a partner with one of the world's biggest global headhunters, Spencer Stuart. Along the way, Jan has been made an honorary professor of the Warwick Business School and elected to the Institute of Directors Council. She also is a director of two quoted companies. To start with, the tour operator and package holiday company First Choice Holidays, where she is the senior non-executive director. Then in 1998 she also joined as a non-executive director at the fledgling medical company Veos. This company is entrepreneurial and has joined the Alternative Investment Market to raise funds for its idea of introducing the Oves, a revolutionary new contraceptive for women, on a global basis.

At a City gathering organised for the Breakthrough breast cancer charity, Jan Hall alluded to the difficulties of getting women and their concerns recognised by saying: 'It will be very difficult, until you get more senior women around in companies, to get breasts into the boardroom'. Asked about what she thinks about women's qualities she says: 'Women make extremely good directors. As a generalisation, they are open, good at challenging old perceptions and good at listening.'

From her job and her role on the ruling body of the IOD, she has noticed that women have been working harder to develop themselves and improve their qualifications for top jobs. But, Jan Hall sees it still as a lonely environment and she sees the need for successful women to help others along.

Jan Hall decided to move into headhunting because she recognised it was an area of business that was going to take off. 'I could see it would be one of the growth industries of the next decade.' Her firm, despite being one of the biggest in the world with representation in 48 countries, has a very flat management structure in the UK. The partners are 'paid very well', but, unlike the manager partners of firms of solicitors, senior partners in headhunters tend to be hands-on.

The skills needed to be a successful headhunter are very different to those needed in running a large multinational business.

For the future, Jan says about her aspirations: 'It is not inconceivable that I could lead a company again. But it won't be because I have been a headhunter.'

♀

'Headhunting is very hard work', says Jan. 'It is an important, fun and interesting business. However, it is work in which you have an element of control in how you do it and sometimes a choice of when you do it. Some people have fun and call it a Martini job . . . a job that you can do 'any place', 'anywhere' and 'any time!', says Jan.

This element of control is something that Jan says is difficult to achieve at the very highest level in more mainstream businesses. 'The work culture is a real problem for many working mothers. For women it can mean you are away from the home too long. For many women, the pressure to achieve in the workplace and be "mummy" at home is a hard balance to strike. Despite some men now spending more time with their families and a few being the main carer, by and large, it is women who have to, and importantly want to, juggle work and family. In smaller businesses, many women take a lead role, but in big businesses, right at the top women are still rare', says Jan. Jan thinks this is a mix of 'glass ceilings' not being cracked and male dominated cultures. But it is also a function of the fact that women both perceive they have, and often do have, a choice. Many choose to exercise it, in favour of a balanced life, rather than the boardroom.

'From the women's perspective, it can be very hard work', says Jan. 'The work culture is a real problem. For women it means you are away from the home too long. We should be championing a culture where no one works for more than 40 hours a week.

Men do have advantages. Obviously, men do not have to have career breaks when children appear. But, for potential go-getters in the business world, there are other more subtle barriers to women in leading international organisations. In the jet-set age, airlines still do not allow mothers-to-be on the planes. So women bosses cannot spend days away to justify clinching a deal on the other side of the world in the same way that a top man can.'

When Jan Hall was climbing the career path, while at the same time as having young children, she says she was forced into 'making serious compromises' and looking back there were times when she considered herself to be 'a bad mother'. 'Having children alters the way you measure success for yourself.' In other words, having a three-year-old at home did eat away at Jan's motivation for work. 'In terms of progress for women into boardrooms, it has been a case of slowly, slowly, catchy monkey. But we could be catching the wrong monkey. It is of course true to say that things are much better than they used to be. However, it is depressing we have managed to do it in a way, by and large, that has not factored in a life outside work for either men or women', says Jan.

'Some of the people who reach the very top are flawed personalities. This is part of the reason for their success. But, many do so at huge personal cost – the saddest thing for women and all too often men, is to step off, or be forced down the corporate ladder at the end of their careers to discover they have no life outside work and having to face the question "was it all worth it?" For women, a small baby or a demanding child often ensures they ask themselves that question, before it is too late', says Jan.

'That does not mean I'm not seduced by the challenge of it', says Jan, indicating that there is a buzz attached to winning recognition in business that can even be intoxicating enough to outweigh the excitements of motherhood.

# 14

# *The Way Forward*

There is a growing group of 'Power Women' in this country. It is a band that is making its presence felt in business, in Westminster, in the media, in the ranks of the police and the legal profession and among the 'great and good'.

It may well also be true that 'Girl Power' has not only arrived, but been blessed with credibility. How come? In the year 2000, for the first time, girls had some proof for boasts of being more intelligent than their male classmates. In 'A' Levels and degree results, girls grabbed the top grades from the boys in our schools and universities.

We know that entrepreneurial women are now heading a third or more of all business start-ups. These entrepreneurial women are driven by the desire to be 'creators of jobs'. They also work with customer satisfaction at the forefront of their minds, rather than being driven by an over-riding personal motivation of being 'wealth creators'. There has been an increasing percentage of women who make it to the boardrooms of our biggest corporations, but, there is a way to go before this percentage reflects the fact that more than half of our brightest graduates, from all subjects, are women.

The United States has been more fertile ground for women entrepreneurs than the UK. True enough, this country's female business champions are catching up. But, for too long, those few who make it to the very top have come from across the Atlantic. Texan, Marjorie Scardino, remains the lone woman chief executive of a FTSE 100 group. She has risen far on merit and even ranks above The Queen and the influential PM's wife, Cherie Blair, in a list of the most powerful people in the country. Scardino has interesting guidance for those aspiring to follow in her footsteps, with advice like 'Have a plan, execute it violently, and do it today'.

In the City, where hostility and harassment has been rife, there are also signs of women winning more top jobs. Nicola Horlick has earned the label 'superwoman' for the way she has determinedly risen to the peak of the fund management world, while simultaneously rearing a handful of children. She is a person like no other. Remember, for instance, how she 'expelled' herself from school at the tender age of 14. She likes to 'pack as much as possible into every minute' and obviously has a calculating and highly intelligent mind that is different to the rest. Nevertheless, she has inspirational qualities for those hoping to change the world of money. Look at what she said when she fought tooth and nail to win her job back at Morgan Grenfell: 'It is quite a female thing, when something is not fair, to stand out and say so. More of a manly reaction would be to shrug shoulders and get on with life.' Also in the world of finance, we can see in the career of Fiona Price how attitudes have softened. When she began in the 1980s, women 'were not desired clients, or seen as decision-makers'. But she now heads a thriving advice firm dominated by women staff and customers.

At Westminster we have seen how a record number of women MPs entered Parliament and how cabinet rank has been given to an unprecedented number from the so-called 'fairer sex'. The challenge remains for them to make a lasting impact beyond 'House-keeping jobs'.

In the legal world, the majority of those who set out as solicitors are women. It is interesting to see how a few, at last, even have made it to senior partner.

The charismatic Barbara Wilding provides an example of one of the handful of women who command very senior posts in our police force. She had to fight ingrained prejudice against women to win promotion. We all can be inspired by what motivated her along the way to being 'Top Cop'. How she looked into the eyes of very wicked criminals and said to herself: 'I'm going to put away this bad guy and stop him roaming the streets again'.

Passion is a very important weapon for those who have made it to the top. In the case of Anita Roddick, her 'green passions' have been lived and breathed alongside her business career. A sheer passion for retailing has helped drive Beverley Hodson at WHSmith to perhaps the most influential and powerful position of any woman in UK retail.

A different kind of passion is helping drive the likes of Martha Lane Fox and those who have floated to the top of public consciousness on the back of revolutionary new ways of doing business. In her case, what helps her 'bounce out of bed' to face 14-hour days as she tries to re-write the environment for holiday and leisure bookings, is the sheer 'excitement' of it all and being head of her own show.

We have seen how the e-commerce revolution is comparable to the 'Wild West of the Gold Rush era'. Those involved have a 'can-do' and positive attitude and really feel they can make the most of their chances. Lucy Marcus, founder of HighTech Women, offers the tip 'Suck the marrow out of every opportunity . . . it might not come round again'.

But, it can never all be rosy. As the founder of another entrepreneurial networking club says: 'Nobody accomplishes anything in life without pain, struggle, energy and drive'.

In the glitzy media world, women have had a longer track record of floating to the top. Nevertheless, one, glossy magazine publisher, Sally O'Sullivan, has interesting tips for those who want to be a 'go-getter' today. 'Work out exactly why you are starting your own business – it's always useful to keep in the back of your mind in the darker moments. Also don't be put off when people tell you how difficult it will be, or how brave you are being.' Sally believes knowing where to go to find answers is more important than trying to know everything yourself. 'You should pull every string you can. Trust your instincts.'

Having the necessary attitude is an essential prerequisite for anyone wanting to make a difference and 'ruffle feathers'.

Take the example of Kate Bleasdale, the former nurse who was feted as a young entrepreneur and who wants to shake up the health business. 'I don't expect people to be nicer, or gentler, to me because I am a woman.' And on the role of women in the business world, she offers the advice: 'Never use your sex as an excuse for not achieving'. 'Anyone doing things innovative and different has to be big enough and strong enough to handle criticism. You have to take the rough with the smooth', she says.

Those women who have broken through in worlds that were traditionally hostile have needed steely determination. But this is a quality that is needed by anyone who really wants to 'make it'. Denise Kingsmill, the successful lawyer turned business regulator, talks about her 'determination to make a difference'. She has been open about her ambition to one day become boss of one of our giant corporations.

Good luck to her. Maybe she will bounce off the 'springboard stage' mentioned by Lady Howe. But this book has also been about the women who are currently lesser known. They may have been unknown to you before reading their stories. But I hope they, and others that follow them, will find it is their 'Time for the Top'.

# Bibliography

The author would like to acknowledge the following sources.

Butler, D. and Butler, G. (2000) *Twentieth-century British Political Facts, 1900–2000*, Palgrave (formerly Macmillan Press).

Davidson, A. (1999) *Management Today*, August.

Davidson, A. (2000) *Management Today*, September (on Barbara Cassani and Denise Kingsmill).

Dennison, H. (2000) *Issues Faced by Senior Businesswomen and how they use Networking*, London University.

Horlick, N. (1998) *Can You Really Have It All?*, Pan.

Laurance, B. and Buckingham, L. (2000) 'The king and queen of fund managers', *Financial Mail on Sunday*, July

Mail on Sunday (2000) 'Britian's 100 highest paid women', *Night & Day Magazine*, August.

McDougall, L. (1998) *Westminster Women*, Vintage.

McRae, S. (1996) *Women at the Top*, The Hansard Society.

*Media Guardian* (1997) August (on Marjorie Scardino).

*Media Guardian* (2000) August (on Eve Pollard).

Mills, E. (1998) *Sunday Times*, July (on Penny Hughes).

*Observer* (2000) 'The Power 300 List', October.

Opportunity Now and Catalyst (2000) *Breaking the Barriers – Women in Senior Management in the UK*.

O'Sullivan, S. (1998) 'When the best company is your own', *Mail on Sunday, You Magazine*, October.

Pearson, A. (1997) 'Jolly well will have it all', *Daily Telegraph*, September.

*Sunday Express* (2000) 'There is something about Martha', March (on Martha Lane Fox).

*Sunday Times* (1997) 'Who runs British business?', October.

*Sunday Times* (2000) 'The Sunday Times Rich List', March.

# Index

# Index